ENTERTAINMENT BRINGS SOCIAL ECONOMY INFLUENCE

JOHN LOK

ISBN 979-888606011-9

Contents

Preface

Introduction

In global service industry, entertainment industry has high market share in overall industries. entertainment industry may include: hotel, tourism, movie, music, sport, publishing, electronic playing game etc. these main several aspects. Human must need any kinds of entertainment, for example, liking reading people who must go to book stores or enter e-publishing stores to buy any paper books or e-books to read. Otherwise, like sport or enjoyment tourism people, who must choose to spend time to play any football, basketball or swimming etc. different kinds of sports or going to travel agents to pay money to buy air tickets to choose anywhere to travel.

Hence, due to human needs any kinds of entertainment to enjoy our lives, instead of working. If any entertainment businessmen can predict whether what factors will influence general entertainment consumers' entertainment choices change as well as they can predict why and how their entertainment consumption of kinds change. Then, their entertainment businesses can have much accurate prediction to any kinds of entertainment consumers' behaviors.

This book explains how to apply demand and supply conept to analyze why and how the different kinds of entertainment consumers' entertainment needs changes on above entertainment kinds of markets.

Prologue

Table of content

CHAPTER ONE

How applying economy theories solve economic problems

The economic problem – sometimes called the basic or central economic problem – asserts that an economy's finite resources are insufficient to satisfy all human wants and needs. Economics involves the study of how to allocate resources in conditions of scarcity However, viewing economics as the study of how society allocates resources can lead to conflation of normative economic planning and empirical study of how economic agents operate in these conditions.

In mainstream neoclassical economics, it is assumed that humans pursue their self-interest, and that the market mechanism best satisfies the various wants different individuals might have. These wants are often divided into individual wants (which depend on the individual's preferences and purchasing power parity) and collective wants (which are the wants of entire groups of people). Things such as food and clothing can be classified as either wants or needs, depending on what type and how often a good is requested.

However, economists have sometimes characterized "how" to produce as a "technological problem" of efficiency whereas the allocation of what is produced is an "economic problem". In a free market, the "how" of production and allocation of resources is distributed among economic agents. In a centrally planned economy, a principal decides how and what to produce on behalf of agents. Modern economies are often welfare capitalist with various regulations, which makes the economic system more equitable while retaining the distributed free market system. Due to human wants are unlimited, an infinite series of human wants remains continue with human life. Nobody can claim that all of his wants have been satisfied and he has no need to satisfy any further want. Everybody feels hunger at a time then other he needs water. Sometime one feels the desire of clothing then starts to feel the desire of having good conveyance. When all existing wants are satisfied then new wants starts to create in mind, so the series of wants remains continue till the last moment of life. So an economic problem arises because of existence of unlimited human wants.

● Problem of allocation of resources

The problem of allocation of resources arises due to the scarcity of resources, and refers to the question of which wants should be satisfied and which should be left unsatisfied. In other words, what to produce and how much to produce. More production of a good implies more resources required for the production of that good, and resources are scarce. These two facts together mean that, if a society decides to increase production of some good, it has to withdraw some resources from the production of other goods. In other words, more production of a desired commodity can be made possible only by reducing the quantity of resources used in the production of other goods.

The problem of allocation deals with the question of whether to produce capital goods or consumer goods. If the community decides to produce capital goods, resources must be withdrawn from the production of consumer goods. In the long run, however, [investment] in capital goods augments the production of consumer goods. Thus, both capital and consumer goods are important. The problem is determining the optimal production ratio between the two.

In fact, in our societies, resources are scarce and it is important to use them as efficiently as possible. Thus, it is essential to know if the production and distribution of national product made by an economy is maximally efficient. The production becomes efficient only if the productive resources are utilized in such a way that any reallocation does not produce more of one good without reducing the output of any other good. In other words, efficient distribution means that redistributing goods cannot make anyone better off without making someone else worse off. (See Pareto efficiency.) So, scientists will apply efficient distribution methods to help any countries to earn the absolute advantages when we buy and sell any kinds of products or food between ourselves countries, e.g. when US has good natural resource to grow any food, e.g. potato, wheat , vegetable, cotton , then

US can export to sell to China, because China has no any farms to grow agriculture food to supply itself Chinese to eat. So, China must need to buy any agriculture food from US. Otherwise, China has cheap labor to supply to US any manufacturers to help them to manufacture their electronic products. SO, it has many US factories are built in China to let Chinese workers help them to produce their products because their wages are cheaper to compare US workers. So, comparative economic advantage will be choice to apply between US and China both countries. (Absolute advantage trade theory)

The inefficiencies of production and distribution exist in all types of economies. The welfare of the people can be increased if these inefficiencies are ruled out. Some cost must be incurred to remove these inefficiencies. If the cost of removing these inefficiencies of production and distribution is more than the gain, then it is not worthwhile to remove them.

● The problem of full employment of resources

In view of how to use available resources are fully utilized is an important one. A community should achieve maximum satisfaction by using the scarce resources in the best possible manner—not wasting resources or using them inefficiently. There are two types of employment of resources:

(1) Labour-intensive

(2) Capital-intensive

In capitalist economies, however, available resources are not fully used. In times of depression, many people want to work but can't find employment. It supposes that the scarce resources are not fully utilized in a capitalistic economy.

● The problem of economic growth

If productive capacity grows, an economy can produce progressively more goods, which raises the standard of living. The increase in productive capacity of an economy is called economic growth. There are various factors affecting economic growth. The problems of economic growth have been discussed by numerous growth models, including the Harrod-Domar model, the neoclassical growth models of Solow and Swan, and the Cambridge growth models of Kaldor and Joan Robinson. This part of the economic problem is studied in the economies of development.

● Needs and wants problems

Needs are things or material items of peoples need for survival, such as food, clothing, housing, and water. Everyone has a different needs and wants. Until the Industrial Revolution, the vast majority of the world's population struggled for access to basic human needs.

Wants are effective desires for a particular product, or for something that can only be obtained by working for it. While the fundamental needs of survival are key in the function of the economy, wants are the driving force that stimulates demand for goods and services. To curb the economic problem, economists must classify the nature and different wants of consumers, as well as prioritize wants and organize production to satisfy as many wants as possible.

● Five bases problems of economy

In our societies , in general, our societies will have these similar problems The following points highlight the five basic problems of an economy. The problems are: 1. What to Produce and in What Quantities? 2. How to Produce these Goods? 3. For whom is the Goods Produced? 4. How Efficiently are the Resources being utilized? 5. Is the Economy Growing?.

Problem 1:What to Produce and in What Quantities?

The first central problem of an economy is to decide what goods and services are to be produced and in what quantities. This involves allocation of scarce resources in relation to the composition of total output in the economy. Since resources are scarce, the society has to decide about the goods to be produced: wheat, cloth, roads, television, power, buildings, and so on. Once the nature of goods to be produced is decided, then their quantities are to be decided. How many tones of wheat, how many televisions, how many million of power, how many buildings, etc. Since the resources of the economy are scarce, the problem of the nature of goods and their quantities has to be decided on the basis of priorities or preferences of the society.

If the society gives priority to the production of more consumer goods now, it will have less in the future. A higher priority on capital goods implies less consumer goods now and more in the future. But since resources are scarce, if some goods are produced in larger quantities, some other goods will have to be produced in smaller quantities. Suppose the economy produces capital goods and consumer goods. In deciding the total output of the economy, the society has to choose that combination of capital goods and consumer goods which is in keeping with its resources.

Problem 2: How to Produce these Goods?

The next basic problem of an economy is to decide about the techniques or methods to be used in order to produce the required goods. This problem is primarily dependent upon the availability of resources within the economy. If land is available in abundance, it may have extensive cultivation. If land is scarce, intensive methods of cultivation may be used. If labour is in abundance, it may use labour- intensive techniques; while in the case of labour shortage, capital-intensive techniques may be used.

The technique to be used also depends upon the type and quantity of goods to be produced. For producing capital goods and large outputs, complicated and expensive machines and techniques are required. On the other hand, simple consumer goods and small outputs require small and less expensive machines and comparatively simple techniques.

Further, it has to be decided what goods and services are to be produced in the public sector and what goods and services in the private sector. But in choosing between different methods of production, those methods should be adopted which bring about an efficient allocation of resources and increase the overall productivity in the economy.

Problem 3. For whom is the Goods Produced?

The third basic problem to be decided is the allocation of goods among the members of the society. The allocation of basic consumer goods or necessities and luxuries comforts and among the household takes place on the basis of among the distribution of national income. Whosoever possesses the means to buy the goods may have then. A rich person may have a large share of the luxuries goods, and a poor person may have more quantities of the basic consumer goods he needs.

Problem 4: How Efficiently are the Resources being Utilised?

This is one of the important basic problems of an economy because having made the three earlier decisions, the society has to see whether the resources it owns are being utilized fully or not. In case the resources of the economy are lying idle, it has to find out ways and means to utilize them fully.

Problem 5: Is the Economy Growing?

The last and the most important problem is to find out whether the economy is growing through time or is it stagnant. If the economy is stagnant at any point inside the production possibility curve, it has to be moved on to the production possibility curve PP whereby the economy now produces larger quantities of consumer goods and capital goods. Economic growth takes place through a higher rate of capital formation which consists of replacing existing capital goods with new and more productive ones by adopting more efficient production techniques or through innovations.

All of these economy problems will be our societies often causes to anyone feels need to solve problems in order to achieve our societies can have enough resources to satisfy our every day living.

● The Consumer Problem

Consumer theory is concerned with how a rational consumer would make consumption decisions. What makes this problem worthy of separate study, apart from the general problem of choice theory, is its particular structure that allows us to derive economically meaningful results. The structure arises because the consumer's choice sets are assumed to be defined by certain prices and the consumer's income or wealth. The consumer's problem is to choose that is most preferred or, equivalently, that has the greatest utility.

The assumption of perfect information is built deeply into the formulation of this choice problem, just as it is in the underlying choice theory. Some alternative models treat the consumer as rational but uncertain about the products, for example how a particular food will taste or a how well a cleaning product will perform. Some goods may be experience goods which the consumer can best learn about by trying ("experiencing") the good. In that case, the consumer might want to buy some now and decide later whether to buy more. That situation would need a different formulation. Similarly, if the agent thinks that high price goods are more likely to perform in a satisfactory way, that, too, would suggest quite a different formulation. Agents are price-takers. The agent takes prices p as known, fixed and exogenous. This assumption excludes things like searching for better prices or bargaining for a discount.

Hence , it seems that economic problems and consumer problems are similar, I feel that it is possible , economists can attempt to apply any economic theories to solve some consumer problems in some situations. They can find the accurate solutions when they can apply the suitable economic theories to solve the suitable consumer or economic problems in our societies. I shall indicate that how economists can apply the suitable economic theories to attempt to solve some consumer problems in our societies as below:

Demand And Supply Theory Solves Consumer Problems

What is economy rule predict consumer behaviour? Why and How does economist can apply economy rule to predict consumer behaviours? I shall explain the reasons as below:

Why does economic principle be the best to predict consumer behaviour. It may include these two reasons: The first focuses on the substantive domain of study, in this interpretation , economics is a social science devoted to understanding how the economy works. The second definition focuses on methods: economics is a way of doing social science, using particular tools. In this interpretation the discipline is associated with formal modelling and statistical analysis rather than particular hypotheses or theories about the economy. Therefore, economic methods can be applied to many other areas besides the economy, everything from decisions within the family to questions about political institutions.

● Demand and supply principle predict public transport tool passenger behaviour

Economists need to use the right economic ideas to predict consumer behaviour. So, Misuse the wrong economy ideas to predict consumer behaviours. It will do more wrong judgement to evaluate or predict why and how and when the country's consumer behaviours will change. It is every economist needs to consider issue. For example, the economy idea application of economic supply-demand principles to public transport. Different fares would give commuters with more-flexible hours the incentive to avoid peak travel times. They would allow passenger traffic to spread out over time, reducing the pressure on the public transport system when enabling even larger total passenger flow. IT aims to reduce traffic congestion, increased public-transport use, reduced car-bon emissions and cause air pollution and generated considerable revenue for the country's transport system. So, if the country can apply supply and demand economic principle to attempt to predict how many passengers number needs to catch transport tools to go to work or go to school or other activities. Then, it can predict how many bus, ferry, taxi, train, underground train, tram etc. different public transport tools to satisfy future public transport passengers' needs in society. So, this demand and supply principle is the comparative best rule to predict any kinds of public transport passengers' road needs, when they need to either go to school, go to office, go to leisure or shopping etc. different kinds of activities. So, applying the demand and supply principle to predict road and sea public transport passengers can help the country to reduce air pollution when they feel that they can find any public transport tools to catch any time conveniently , then it can encourage them to reduce car purchase desire. When many people choose to catch public transport tools, then it will reduce many cars number on the road. Then, air pollution will reduce as well as any public transport tools' income will also increase as well as traffic jam will also reduce. When the country can evaluate how many people choose to catch bus or taxi or ferry or train or underground train, or tram or train etc. different kinds of public transport tools, then the country can predict the more accurate public transport tools number to every kind of public transport tool to satisfy their journey needs. e.g. whether underground train or train or tram need to decrease or increase the frequent times or number to catch the volume of passenger in busy or non-busy time; or whether bus company has need to increase how much buses to catch the city location passengers when they are living in the city. Moreover, supply and demand principle can help any public transport tools to explain why their passengers number reduces in the year, it may due to fare charge is unreasonable, feeling uncomfortable to sit on the seat or air condition is poor in the transport tool environment, or there are no more seats because many there are much time is full passenger and no seat vacancy to provide to them to sit . So, supply and demand principle can help any kinds of public transport tools to find whether which is (are) the factor(S) can influence the current or last year passengers number reduce. Then, they can concentrate on improving their weaknesses to raise their service quality . So, supply and demand principle can also help they to evaluate whether what their weakness are in order to improve to increase passengers number. They can do questionnaires to enquiry their passengers' response to evaluate whether which areas of services that they feel unsatisfactory. So, the different kinds of service satisfactory feeling to the passengers number data will be the main source to help the kind of public transport tool to analyse and conclude the results more accurate, then they can make the more accurate judgement to improve the of service. For example, the questionnaires indicate that the many passengers feel the bus fare is reasonable, but many passengers feel they can not find any seats to sit easily. So, it implies that the bus firm ought buy more buses or enlarges bus size and increases more seats in the enlarged buses. Then, it does not reduce its fare but it needs to find solutions to let passengers can find seats to sit in every bus more easily. But, if the questionnaires indicate that there are many passengers feel its fare is higher or unreasonable to compare other kinds of public transportation tools. Hence, it can avoid to spend more expenditure to increase bus number to the city, if the city has many passengers , they still choose bus to catch, but they feel its fare is too higher to compare other kinds of public transport tool. Then, it only needs to reduce its fare , it ought help it to increase passengers number. Hence, demand and supply principle is the most suitable economic method to evaluate any kinds of public transport system passenger needs in any country nowadays.

● Supply and demand and price elasticities principle predict oil energy user behaviour

The another case is that demand and supply principle can predict oil buyer behaviour to find whether what factors can cause the oil buyer individual need reduces. For example , a rise in production costs increases market prices and reduces quantities demanded and supplied. Or when, energy cost rise, utility bills increases and households fid extra ways of saving heating and electricity. But, others are nor. For example, whether a tax is imposed on the producers or consumer of a commodity, say oil has nothing to do with who ends up paying for it. The tax might be administered on oil companies, but it might be consumers who really pay for it through higher prices at the pump. Or the extra cost might be imposed on consumers in the form of a sale tax, but the oil companies might be forces to absorb it through lower prices. It all depends on the " price elasticities" of demand and supply. With the addition of extra assumption, this model also generates rather strong implications about how well markets work. In particular, a competitive market economy is efficient in the sense that it is impossible to improve one person's well-being without reducing somebody.

● Demand and supply principle can misuse to predict consumer behaviour when the two firms participate advertisement to promote their products in the same time

Why can demand and supply principle misuse to predict consumer behaviour when the two firms participate advertisement to promote their products in the same time ? I shall explain as below: Assume that two competing firms must decide whether to have a big advertising budget. Advertising would allow one firm to steal some of the other's customers.

But when they both advertise, the effects on customer demand cancel out. The firms end up having spent money needlessly.

We might expect that neither firm would choose to spend much on advertising, but the model shows that this logic is off base. When the firms make their choices independently and they care only about their own profits, each one has an incentive to advertise, regardless of what the other firm does. When the other firm does not advertise, you can steal customers from it if you do advertise, when the other firm does advertise, you have to advertise to prevent loss of customers. So, these two firms end up in a bad equilibrium in which both have to waste resources. This market can not apply demand and supply principle to predict consumer behaviours because they depends advertisement to promote their products. If these two firms advertise their products in the same time. Then , it is not possible that if one firm increases it price and it will cause its customer number loss, due to its advertise can help it to attract customers to consider its product from television or radio or newspapers or magazine promotion channels. So, I suppose that these two firms decide to increase their price, when they advertise their products to let customers to know in the same time. They will not lose their customers or reduce their customers easily. Because their customers can be persuaded to choose to buy their products to compare other similar products in preference. So, their increasing price will not influence their customers number lose easily. It explains that demand and supply principle is not right to this case, so demand and supply principle can misuse to help them to predict consumer behaviours when they advertise their products in the same time. Also, demand and supply principle is not suitable to them to predict consumer behaviours when they advertise their products in the same time. They will do wrong prediction to their consumers purchase desire when they advertise their products in the same time.

ON conclusion, using these demand and supply and price elasticity techniques, economists derive specific prediction for how consumers choose which products to buy, how households save, how firms invest, how workers search for jobs, as well as for how these actions depend on the particulars. They can help them to predict job and consumption behaviours more accurate, it depends on whether the situation is right, such as both competition firms participate to advertise their products in the same time case, it is not right to apply above economic principle to predict consumer behaviours. They will get wrong prediction when they apply this principle to predict consumer behaviours.

However, demand and supply principle can predict below any one of these cases. I shall indicate as below:

The problem of need-based scholarships: Most systems for providing college scholarships are based on some definition of financial needs, with scholarships generally being given only to those students who must need financial help in order to attend school.

Is need, rather than academic ability, the best basic on which to choose those students who are to be encouraged to attend college? Which way of choosing who gets aids is the more just? Which is the more efficient ? Is the overall educational level of society increased more by giving financial aid to bright students or to needy students? Presumably the aid offers more leverage to needy students, since they all need the money in order to attend college, whereas, many of the bright students would attend college in any case. But is a smaller number of bright students the more important addition?

So, the school can apply demand and supply principle to predict whether how many parents feel need financial assistance and evaluate how much financial amount is the right to borrow. It aims to calculate how many parents feel real financial need and how much to lend to them in order to let these students to get the most fair financial assistance.

Assuming the school wish to use need as a basis, how does the school determines " financial need"?

Is need a function or parents' income? What, then , does the school about children of wealthy parents who are living independently of them and get no aid from parents? Should they be punished for their parents' wealth? But if they are given aid, won't all students, in order to get aid, claim to be independent of their parents?

Is need solely a matter of family income, or should not the school takes a family's financial obligations into account? Does not it make more sense to give aid to someone whose parents must put night more children through school than to someone from a family of five or one only with the same income? But in a possible parallel situations, should a family that carries mortgages on one or two large homes get preference simply because they do not have much money left to spend on college? Does doing this reward ? Is there a difference between the case of night children and the case of the large mortgage? How should parents who are not married , but are living together and supporting their children jointly be counted? Most parents are supporter to their children , although they are married in possible.

So, the school needs to gather all these data to evaluate how many parents are not married or married or living with their children together, how much salary they earn as well as every family has how much children as well as whether they have mortgage for their houses. So, these number will be the financial education assistance demanders, but it does not represent their real financial needs. It is possible that someone does not feel any financial need, although their children apply financial assistance to your school. Then , your school needs to evaluate whether how much financial assistance can lend to every real financial need student family. It can not exceed your final financial expenditure budget (supply) , when your financial expenditure is not enough. SO, demand and supply principle can be applied to research this school real family financial demand to lend to the real financial need families and evaluate whether the reasonable financial amount to lend to every child family to study in your school.

● Supply and demand principle applies to immigration to decide wage case

A fascinating and important example of supply and demand, full of complexities, is the role of immigration in determining wages. If you ask people , they are likely to tell you that immigration into California or Florida US, surely lowers the wages of people in those regions. It is just supply and demand analysis of immigration. According to this analysis, of these to these two regions in US. Immigration in to a region shifts the supply curve for labor to the right and pushes down wages. Why has it relationship between immigration to US these two regions immigrant number and wage?

Careful economic studies cast doubt on this simple proposition, however, a recent survey of the evidence concludes:

The effect of immigration on the labor market outcomes of natives is small in US. There is no evidence of economically significant reductions in native employment. Most analysis, finds that a 10 percent increase in the fraction of immigrants in the population reduced native wages by a most 1%.

How can we explain the small impact of immigration on wages? The main mistake is to forget how mobile the American population is and that the impact of immigration on wages, we must examine the effect of new immigrants when the strength of the local economy and the number of native-born residents in a city are unchanged, that is , when these other things are held constant. Unless you exclude the effects other changing variables, you can not accurately predict the impact of immigration. The same principle holds in doing a supply0and demand analysis of any market. As much as possible, when you are examining the impact of a supply or demand shift, you must try to keep all other things constant.

● Rationing by prices

By determining the equilibrium prices and quantities of all inputs and outputs, the market allocated or rations out the scare goods of the society among the possible uses. Who does the rationing? A planning board? Congress or the president? BO, the marketplace, through the interaction of supply and demand, doe the rationing. This is rationing by the purse.

What foods are produces? This is answered by the signals of the market price. High oil prices stimulates oil production, whereas low food prices drive resources out of agriculture. Those who have the most dollars votes have the greatest influences on what goods are produced. All of these considers how demand and supply to the market.

For whom are goods produces? The power of the pursue indicates the distribution of income and consumption. Those with higher incomes end up with larger houses, more clothing, and linger vacations. When the most urgently felt needs get fulfilled through the demand curve.

Even, the how question is decided by supply and demand. When corn prices are low, it is not profitable for farmers to use expensive tractors and irrigation systems, and only the best land is cultivated. When oil prices are high, oil companies drill in deep offshore waters and employ novel seismic techniques to find oil.

IN sum , any thing needs through demands, interact with costs of goods, as reflected in supplies in our economic world. Hence, demand and supply theory ought be the most accurate method to help any businesses or governments to predict their shareholders behaviours when they will change as well as how and how their behaviours change.

Consumer choice theory solves consumer problems

What is 'consumer choice theory'?

'Consumer choice theory' is a hypothesis about why people buy things. Put simply, it says that you choose to buy the things that give you the greatest satisfaction, while keeping within your budget. At the heart of this theory are three assumptions about human nature.[1]

The first assumption is that when you shop, you choose to buy things based on calculated decisions about what will make you happiest. In economics language, this is known as utility maximisation (Economists really like to put quite simple concepts into long complicated terms.)

Secondly, the theory assumes that no matter how much you shop, you will never be completely satisfied. In other words, you will always be happier consuming a little bit more. This is known as the principle of non-satiation. Thirdly, even though you always get more happiness from more consumption, the amount of pleasure you get from each good decreases with the more you consume. So if you eat two ice creams rather than one, you get more overall pleasure, but the second ice-cream won't be as satisfying as the first. This is known as decreasing marginal utility.

Consumer choice theory has influenced everything from government policy to corporate advertising to academia. But the theory has been criticized for not being the most accurate description of how people actually make choices. A whole new branch of economics, called 'behavioral economics', has emerged essentially to use findings from psychology to disprove the assumptions behind consumer choice theory. This has also led others to argue that consumer choice theory is less about describing how we do actually behave, and is more about describing how people should behave.[3] In other words, by portraying people as self-interested shopaholics, economists are saying that is it okay and natural for us to be avid consumers.

● Consumer choice theory can be applied to solve consumer problems during the country can have economic growth , the reasons may include as below:

The scenario leading to inflation starts with poor growth. Forget about everything that comes next and focus on that most important factor. Because it happens that the scenario leading to a budget crisis also starts with poor growth, and the scenario leading to a long-term unemployment crisis starts with poor growth, and a scenario leading to a better-the-neighbor trade crisis starts with poor growth, and so on. So a very important question is: what can be done to improve the prospects for economic growth? In particular, what is the right countercyclical approach to take to best situate the economy for future growth? I shall indicate during US, America's economy growth occurs, then economists can attempt to apply customer choice theory to solve US itself country's consumer problems more easier.

In no small part, the question comes down to interpretations of charts like the one at right. On the one hand, long and deep downturns seem to have almost no effect on the long-term rate of growth. On the other hand, in the long run we're all dead, and those who live during an extended period of economic weakness suffer for it. Meanwhile, it's also difficult to see where high debt levels influence the long-run rate of growth, at least where this chart is concerned.

During to the medium-term growth stage, is the bigger threat to American growth rates a market revolt against American debt levels? Or is it structural unemployment stemming from the slow, jobless recovery? Or is the cyclical shortfall in public investment? Or something else entirely? Of course, there's no real reason one has to choose a problem to address at the expense of others. More aggressive monetary expansion could make the finding of a solution to all these problems easier, but the Fed is unwilling to oblige me on this score. It may well be concerned that lack of fiscal discipline will lead to increasing inflation expectations, making its job harder (but then fiscal problems are trace able to growth). If that is the worry, however, one has to ask why the Congress has been unable to strike a deal for $20 billion in stimulus this year for $80 billion in fiscal tightening in a year or two (fill in whatever amounts you wish). But the outlook for the American economy vis-a-vis any number of potential crises will hinge on growth, and growth will hinge on the ability of private business to exploit promising opportunities as they arise. And the question is: what's likely to hurt that ability most? High interest rates? Lack of consumer demand? A shortage of adequately prepared workers? Right now firms appear to be most worried about demand shortfalls. So how much can you boost demand without making the primary fear high interest rates? A lot, if the expansion is on the monetary side.

● How to supply consumer choice theory to predict Consumer Behavior Marketing at Apple Computer

During US economy growth, Apply computer applies consumer choice theory to solve its computer buyers' choice problems among different kinds of brand computer competitors. Have you ever wondered why Apple is so successful? They were not the first company to invent the personal computer, portable music device, the tablet, the smartphone, software to download music, or the set-top box to name a few. Apple has amassed a brand loyal following like no other brand backed by significant sales, market share, and profitability. So, how does Apple do it? What's the secret behind their success?

Marketing using consumer behavior insight is how Apple succeeds. Even though Steve Jobs and Apple, did not use consumer research in the initial development of most products, consumer behavior plays a huge role in their marketing and ultimately the success of the company. Once a consumer purchases a product or downloads iTunes Apple has access to data the company leverages. Apple uses this information to gain significant insight into the consumer and what drives purchase behavior.

Consumer behavior marketing is an essential ingredient in the current business climate. The companies that apply this type of marketing well have a distinct competitive advantage that distances them from their rivals. Consumer behavior research is the primary driver at the core of any good strategy. Research provides actionable insight and ensures business success. If you answer no to the following questions, this post is for you?

•Are you applying consumer behavior marketing currently?

•Have you conducted consumer behavior research within the last two years?

•Do you have consumer behavior marketing in your marketing plan with well-defined marketing strategies and tactics?

•Are you achieving the maximum results for your organization?

Every business has a target audience and consumer behavior marketing provides the fundamental methods for understanding your target. Consumer behavior research provides the underlying element that drives quality strategies and ensures business results.

"Marketing is understanding your buyers really, really well. Then creating valuable products, services, and information especially for them to help solve their problems."

The organizations that have an intimate understanding of their target audience possess a competitive advantage over those that do not. Establishing a one-to-one relationship and thorough knowledge of your target audience is a core responsibility for business in the 21st century and beyond. Regardless if you are B2B, B2C, B2G or a hybrid organization you have a target audience. The information in this post can be applied to any business type. This post focuses on Apple (B2C) employing consumer behavior marketing as a critical ingredient for their success.

Hence, Apply computer shops have several computer teachers to teach any visitors how to use its laptops, hen they enquire its any computer salespeople. Due to its salespeople had been trained to learn how to use the different kinds of laptops. So, anyone enquires them, they can answer their enquires concern any computer questions immediately. Then, they will feel Apple laptops are the first choice to compare other kinds of laptops brands. It is one salespeople answering strategies to persuade any Apple computer visitors to feel its any laptops are the first or preference choice to compare its competitors in this computer market, so customer choice economic theory is the most suitable strategy to solve Apple computer's customer individual purchase decision problem.

Microeconomics Models and Theories solve customer problems

Microeconomics is concerned with the economic decisions and actions of individuals and firms. Within the broad church of microeconomics, there are different theories that certain assumptions and expectations of economic behaviour. The most important theory is neo-classical theory, which places emphasis on free-markets and the assumption individuals are rational and seek to maximise utility. However, there are many critiques of the neo-classical model, arguing economics is more complex with issues of market failure and irrational behaviour.

Pre-classical microeconomic theory

Before, Adam Smith, economics was more disparate with no commanding overall theory. Philosophers like Aristotle and Plato made references to issues in economics such as division of labour. The dominant ideas, pre-classical economics, were based on theories of mercantilism – the idea a nation should try to accumulate gold.

Classical microeconomic theory

Classical microeconomic theory was developed by Adam Smith (Wealth of Nations, 1776) and later economists, such as David Ricardo The essential aspect of classical microeconomic theory include:

Adam Smith mentioned the 'invisible hand of the market.' He noted how when people act out of self-interest, markets tend to provide goods and services which are demanded by the population. It needed no central price setting, but market forces responded to changes in demand and supply, e.g. a shortage pushes up the price and causes demand to fall.

Smith also investigated topics such as the division of labour, specialisation and economies of scale. The early classical economists emphasised the importance of costs to firms and consumers.

Utility maximisation

An important development of classical economics towards the end of the nineteenth century is the concept of utility maximisation. The concept of utility was developed by philosophers/economists – Jeremy Bentham and John Stuart Mill. In microeconomic theory, it was believed a consumer will buy goods depending on the marginal utility (satisfaction) they get from the good. This theory assumes consumers are rational and seeking to maximise the satisfaction they get.

Neo-classical theory

Neo-classical theory is a modern re-interpretation of classical economics of the nineteenth century. Neo-classical theory places importance on markets, but developed new ideas, especially regarding utility and rational choice theory. Elements of neo-classical theory.

1. Market distribution of goods and services.

2.R ational choice theory. This is the idea individuals hold rational preferences and make rational choices; seeking to maximise their outcomes – be it profit, wages, consumption or investment.

3. People act independently and make use of available information.

4. Marginalism. In neo-classical economics, more emphasis was placed on concepts of marginal utility and marginal cost. We make choices depending on satisfaction we get from one extra unit of a good.

Economists such as Carl Menger, William Stanley Jevons and Marie-Esprit-Léon Walras. and Alfred Marshall developed ideas such as diminishing marginal utility. Many of these neo-classical economic theories were brought together in Alfred Marshall's very influential textbook, Principles of Economics. (1890)

•Note there is some blurring between classical economics and neo-classical economics.

•Neo-classical economics has also come to mean 'orthodox economic theory. To a large extent, it has incorporated new developments in microeconomics, such as theories of market failure, market structure and econometrics.

Theories of Market failure

Neo-classical economics has become associated with a belief in the efficiency of markets. However, microeconomic theory has also incorporated the criticisms and limitations of free-markets.

•Monopoly. Adam Smith was well aware of the problem of monopolies and how firms could use their market power to set excessive prices.

•Imperfect competition. In the 1930s, Joan Robinson developed a model of imperfect competition, an awareness many markets were somewhere between monopoly and perfect competition often assumed in neo-classical economics.

•Externalities. Developed by Arthur C.Pigou in The Economics of Welfare (1920) this is the awareness production and consumption decisions can have harmful (or positive) effects on third parties. Therefore, a free market can lead to overconsumption of demerit goods and negative externalities.

•Game theory. An awareness, decisions are not linear or simple, but the interdependence of agents influences what we decide to do.

Behavioural economics

The most important trend in recent decades in economics is the greater emphasis placed on aspects of behavioural economics, which uses many insights from related fields such as psychology.

•Disputes rational choice theory. The essential element of behavioural economics is that it argues individual agents are often not rational and often do not seek to maximise utility.

•Behavioural economics examines how agents can be influenced by biases, and make decisions not predicted by neo-classical economic theory. Behavioural economics can explain the irrational exuberance of booms and busts.

Econometrics

In the post-war period, economics became increasingly mathematical with economists attempting to use mathematics to explain models and theories. Econometrics looks at economic data and seeks to extract simple relationships. The basic tool is the linear regression models and can be used to try and predict consumer spending and demand for labour.

Heterodox models of microeconomics

Heterodox models differ substantially from microeconomic foundations of neo-classical economics. Schools of thought include

Marxist economic theory

Karl Marx developed an alternative perspective on economics. He focused on the surplus value created under the capitalist economic system. To Marx, the invisible hand of the market would be better described as the invisible hand of capitalist exploitation of workers. Marx claimed workers did receive their full labour value but were compensated for their necessary labour only – enabling capitalists to profit from the surplus.

Institutional economics. The role of society and institutions in shaping economic behaviour. For example, Thomas Veblen looked at theories of 'conspicuous consumption' and noted how the desire for social status could drive much economic theory. Institutional economics could be seen as a forerunner for later behavioural economics.

Environmental economics Argues traditional economics wrongly places value on increasing output. The most important thing is creating a sustainable environment which maximises living standards. So, manufacturers need to consider how to manufacture their products , but pollution can not be raised as the same time, because human will face to raise cost of living and living experiences to be poor , even food shortage, water pollution , air pollution , death rate raises when technological productivities brings pollution to our natural environment. Hence, environmental economoic theory is the most suitable to solve manufacturers' pollution problem.

Buddhist economics/non-profit goals. Like environmental economics, this questions the assumption higher incomes and higher output are desirable. The theory of hedonistic relativism suggests higher incomes do nothing to increase happiness levels, and traditional economics can encourage society to pursue materialistic goals which actually create more problems of stress, conflict and environmental degradation.

Some of the basic models you might find in A-Level economics :

•Price Discrimination

•Perfect competition

•Price Mechanism

•Monopoly

•Oligopoly and kinked demand curve

•Game Theory Pricing strategies

•Market failure

•Behavioural economics

ON conclusion, any macro economy theories can be applied to find the most reasonable methods to solve any customer problems in societies by economists as above. So, I believe that any economic and customer and social problems can be solved by economic theories in our society.

Demand and supply theory solves social problems

Over the past 20 years, many researchers believe to apply behavioral economic macroeconomic models which can predict market behavioral change. The reasons are based on assumptions of optimizing behavior in many cases have difficulty accounting for key real-world observations. Hence, researchers have used behavioral economics assumptions with the aim of making their model predicting better fit the data. The reason for behavioral economics results into macroeconomics will be more accurate to predict market behavioral change in macro-economy view point, such as economic fluctuation prediction, the consumption, formation of expectations and determination of wages and employment how to aggregation supply and the possibility of consumer individual demand product or service number prediction more accurately.

● How to apply behavioral economy (demand and supply) theory to predict marketing behavioral changes more accurate?

Anyway, economists aim to develop models of human behavior and interactions in market in order to build useful models. Economists make simplifying assumptions to analyze why the market will be changed by consumer individual consumption behavior changing.

Why do I assume consumers are as economic man ? In behavioral economy view point, how the perception of the economic man's behavior (including consumer choices) of economic models with the development of economics as a science. Economists explain the concept of economics as a science. It is the concept of consumer as an economic man, the essence and complexity of consumer behavior.

The consumer and consumer purchasing behavior are an important area of interest of many scientific disciplines. The process of economic decision making as well as consumption choices are connected with wider human activities. The terms of both consumer individual attitudes and group social behavior will influence group social behavior will influence consumer individual final consumption decision in every consumption choice process. Thus, behavioral economy method can predict consumer behavioral changing, it can apply these sciences to research, includes sociology, psychology, anthropology, operational research, decision theory etc. different literature research aspects. I assume that businessmen can apply behavioral economy method to predict market changing behaviors successfully if they own behavioral economy knowledge.

In this part, I shall concentrate on explain how the perception of the economic man's behavior (including consumer choice) is applied to predict market behaviors. After explaining the concept of consumer as an economic man, the nature and complexity of consumer behavior are discussed to below different industries' marketing behavioral changing every case studies in US or UK countries.

Why is consumer as an economic man? IN behavioral economy view point, the concept of answer is one of the fundamental concepts in economics because the consumer is the case market participant along with the producer. In general, lecturers define the consumer in various ways, but in behavioral economy view point, consumers mean economy man. Because who will compare cost and benefit to any product or service to decide to choose to buy the product or consume the service. Consumers are as "economic man", who will make own subjective preferences (tastes), habits and traditions and existing objective constraints (i.e. disposal income) market prices of products and services in order to satisfy whose needs to a maximum degree and in the most rational way.

Thus, economic man means consumers need to make psychological mind to decide whether who either prefer to buy this product or another product or prefer to consume this service or another service more suitable. Thus, any markets or industries need have themselves benefits and consumers must need to evaluate whether the product or service has more benefits to compare other products or services in the consumption market to satisfy whose needs. It means that if the product or service has more benefits to compare other similar products or services. Then the product or service will persuade many consumers to choose to but the product or consume the service.

Consequently, in first part, I shall indicate how to apply behavioral economy theory : economic man psychological method, benefits and costs benefits method, how to predict these US and UK enterprises marketing behavioral changing more accurate.

In the second part, I shall apply micro employee behavioral economy concept to explain how to solve these US and UK inter-organizational management challenge.

I believe that behavioral economy method can be applied to research organizational employee behaviors change, e.g. how any why the employee chooses to do this action in whose organization. Moreover, behavioral economy method can be applied to consumption market to predict how any why the consumer choose to buy the product or consume the service. So, any consumers and employees personal psychology and external environment economic factor will influence how to choose to do decision in any organizations or consumption environment.

Bibliography

Bandiera, O., I. Barankay, and I. Rasul (2005). Social preferences and the response to incentives: Evidence from personal data. The quarterly journal of economics 120 (3), 917-969.

Exadaktylos, F., A.M. Espin and P. Branas-Garza (2013). Experimental subjects are not different. Scientific reports 3, 1213.

Lazear, E.P. (1979). Why is there mandatory retirement? Journal of political economy 87(6), 1261-1284.

● Behavioral economic method (demand and supply theory) predicts stable basic income consumer individual spending behavior

Can apply behavioral economic method to predict that the consequences of a stable basic income consumer's consumption behavior? It may be significantly different than the ones are predicted by the standard economic model if more realistic assumptions of human consumption behavioral prediction success.

Behavioral economic method assumes that consumer will compare whether whose benefits are more than costs after they buy the product or consume the service. I assume the consumer is only the who have stable basic income source consumer target. This stable basic income target consumers who will evaluate or feel they will earn more benefits than costs to every product in their consumption process, after they will make final decision to choose to buy the product to use or consume the service. Otherwise, if they feel they won't earn more benefits after they buy the product or consume the service in the consumption process. Then, they won't choose to buy the product to use or consume the service. In behavioral economic view point, it indicates their consumption behaviors are depend on comparing the product or the service whether it can satisfy their desire benefits and their desire benefits to the product or service must be more than their consumption cost.

There are four points to apply behavioral economic method to predict each stable basic income individual income spending. They include: motivation, conspicuous consumption, social preferences and crowding theory.

Each stable basic income consumer individual spending amount will be different and it is represent that every high stable basic income consumer must decide to consume any high cost services or buy high cost products to use. Although some economic teachers assume general high income people will accept to spend more expenditures for enjoyment or buy high cost of products to satisfy basic high level necessary expenditures. But, applying behavioral economic analysis, it is not absolute true, some low income people also accept to spend more to buy high cost of products or increasing spending expenditures for enjoyment for their basic necessary expenditures.

The field of behavioral economic can be fined as a combination of economics and psychology that tries to capture human behavior in a more realistic. Understanding each consumer individual consumption behavior, we need to know how who does each decision to influence each consumption choice. Consequently, analysis reaches the conclusion. Every high or low level stable basic income consumer individual behavioral consumption that the microeconomic consequences of a stable basic income of individual consumer target consumption group could be efficiency enhancing, but at the same time incentives about positional concerns could lead to wasteful and inefficient spending to the stable low basic income consumer target group.

● How to apply demand and supply theory to contribute to the stable basic income target consumer group's consumption prediction?

What is basic income mean? A basic income is an income paid by a political community to all its members on an individual basis, without means test or work requirement. How to apply behavioral economic method to contribute to the basic income consumption prediction?

I assume high income tax is charged to one high income tax payee , it will influence the high income tax payee individual consumption desires to be fallen, also extrinsic incentives will effort and intrinsic motivation and how the labor market change these variables under and big changes predicting, how income security changes social consumption preferences, e.g. how a big change affects the overall level of status -seeking behavior and this effect with income inequality to influence consumer individual consumption attitude or habit.

How can behavioral economic methods predict consumer's consumption decision, in special the stable basic income consumer target group? In any consumption decisions are involving risk and uncertainty, the standard economic model usually assumes that decisions are based on final condition, regardless of the changes are caused by the results of a consumer's decision.

An alterative mode of how consumers make decision and judgement under risk and uncertainty. This situation is often occurred in consumption market.

In behavioral economic view point, it explains how consumer's consumption, however, which excludes the stable basic income earn factor can influence the stable basic income earn target consumer group decides to make final consumption decision to compare to the non-stable basic income earn target consumer group. The reasons include as below:

(1) Consumers evaluate decisions over gains and losses with respect to some natural reference point, when they feel need to consume, which is assumed to be judgement about a sequence of outcomes are based on changes in wealth, rather than whether how much absolute basic income earn to influence whose consumption desires.

(2) Thus, behavioral economic theory assumes the consumer is the low level of income group in society, but when who feels that he is still gains more than losses when who decides to buy the expensive product or consumes the expensive service. Then, the low level of income consumer who will accept to buy the expensive product or consume the service easily. Due to whose gains feeling is more than losses feeling, when who buys the product or consumes the service.

(3) Behavioral economic theory also assumes the taxpayer will pay high income tax in this year. The, even the high income taxpayer can earn high basic income, but due to whom needs to pay high income tax in this year. Then, he/she will reduce much spending, even he/she reduces spending on cheap products or cheap service consumption for enjoyment. This is the taxpayer's economic decision to influence whose consumption behavior, due to the high income tax expenditure factor influences whose consumption behavior to change to be reduced spending expenditures in this year.

How to apply behavioral economic method to predict labor market changing behavior?

Instead of applying behavioral economic method to predict every consumer individual consumption effort. Behavioral economic method can be also be applied to predict every country's labor market changing behavior. Particularly, how salary clerical workers or low wage labor workers should move from one type of job to another based on these factors. They include as below:

Their intrinsic motivation and how their levels of effort would change after this movement, investigates the effects of income security on social preferences in labor market changing behavior, and how cooperation in social contribution is affected when income security is guaranteed, how to predict the role of positional externalities on conspicuous consumption and how would change the incentive to influence consumption. So, it seems that general labor market job changing behaviors will not influenced by external economic environment better or worse changing factor, or salary changing factor etc. different environmental condition changing factors influence to employees' job changing. Generally, employee's job changing behavior is more influenced to persuade who changes job by himself/herself intrinsic motivation negative emotion influence mainly.

How to apply motivation crowding theory to predict labor productivity? One of the main challenges of economic theory is to find what are the optimal incentives that increase productivity of labors. The standing point is usually extrinsic incentive be it is form of monetary compensations for high effort or fine for low effort.

It is a kind method of reward or punishment to increase or decrease number of productivity to every labor. But it can only raise short term number of productivity in possible and it can not guarantee high quality of productivity. So if one employer wants a labor to do more of an activity or with a higher quality, consider paying the labor for working hard on punishing whom if for providing a low level effort.

This idea is that people do not like to work, and therefore they used some sort of compensation for doing a specific activity, and that the more they are paid the harder, they will work. So, payment better compensation is only beneficial to encourage labors to do one specific task or activity in short term. This method can not be suitable to rise long term beneficial productivity and high level quality of production or excellent performance in long term and it can only keep in short term raising productivity and high level quality of production or excellent performance benefits.

Consider paying the labor for working hard on punishing whom if for providing a low level effort. This idea is that people do not like to work, and therefore they used some sort of compensation for doing a specific activity, and that the more they are paid the harder they will work. So, payment better compensation is only beneficial to encourage labors to do one specific task or activity in short term. This method can not be suitable to raise long them beneficial productivity and high quality of products.

However, economists would argue that, is a labor has high intrinsic motivative to perform a task, who will provide a high level of effort without compensation by himself/herself but an even higher level of effort of whom is compensated. If a labor does not have any intrinsic motivation to perform a task or an activity, who will provide no effort or a low effort of whom. There is no compensation, but who will increase this level of effort of an extrinsic incentive is implemented.

Hence, in behavioral economic view point, the labor individual high level effort is a main psychological factor to influence whose productivity to be raised or the qualities of products to be raised, when the products are manufactured by the high level effort labor. It means that high compensation is not the good method to encourage labor productivity or raise quality. Otherwise, how to influence the one low level of effort of labor to change to be one high level of effort labor. It is the best psychological method to influence the labor to raise productivity and quality and service performance to any products or services in manufacturing process or service process for any organizations in long term beneficial possible.

● How can apply demand and supply theory raises basic stable income consumer consumption desire

Economists aim to develop models of human behavior and interactions in consumption markets. But consumers behave in complex ways, such as how to predict consumers to make rational decisions in consumption processes. Moreover, self-consumption control and motivation can vary significantly across different individual consumer.

In order to build useful consumption prediction models, economists make simplifying assumptions, aims to predict how to raise stable basic income consumer target group consumption more success. However, behavioral economy method is one kind of accurate consumption prediction method. It can be applied to predict economic decision-making to every consumer consumption choice more accurate raising whose consumption desire?

I shall indicate how to apply different behavioral economy methods (demand and supply theory) to raise stable basic stable income target consumer group consumption desire in these different consumption situation (consumption environment) aspects as below:

1. Stable basic stable income consumer group consumption great or small amount desire

The consumption of products and services is a fundamental part of consumer's welfare. Basically, every one who has stable basic stable income, who will like to consume any products and services. Even, consumption great or small amount desire won't be depended on whether the person whose income is more or less. It means low income level of people will still like to consume great amount to buy expensive products or consume expensive services, because consumption is human's part of life and basic needs.

This stable basic income people will like to consume, because they have stable income source when they do not worry about unemployment occurrence to cause them have no enough money to support their life. Otherwise, non-stable basic stable income people won't like to consume because they feel they have no stable basic income source to support their life and they will worry about unemployment occurrence any time. Hence, stable basic income people will have more consumption desire to compare non-stable basic stable income people in any countries usually. Behavioral economic method indicates they feel their economic benefits will be loss if they planned to buy any products or consume any services easily. So, they prefer to save money in bank more than consumption.

1. Demand systems and micro-economic factor influence basic income people consumption attitude

Why stable basic income people will like to consume? Because who have more demand, a demand system shows the level of consumer demand for different products and services: e.g. one basic stable income person may refer to the demand for clothes, another the demand for food etc.

How the demand for that particular product varies with the prices and demographic factor will influence who to accept consumption. Such as stable basic income people who will not consider to decide to buy the cloth to wear or the food to eat if who feel the cloth or food price is even more expensive to compare other kind of cloth or food.

Otherwise, non-stable basic income people who will consider to decide to buy the cloth to wear or the food to eat if they feel that they still have enough cloths to wear or enough food to eat at homes , even these food or cloth price are less expensive to compare others. Because they feel they lack stable income effort to support them to consume. Hence, basic stable income factor can influence the consumer's consumption decision.

2. Life-cycle advertisement method can influence consumer individual consumption behaviors to be increased

Consumer behavior makes strong assumptions about the informational and computational bases of consumer behavior. Generally, consumer behavior is reasonably characterized as the maximization of expected lifetime utility subject to budget constraint and conditional on the available information.

Generally, consumers prefer to buy any discounted products or it is reasonable that consumers accept to buy many attractions to persuade them to buy any kinds of bargain discount products. Hence, low bargain discount product is one good behavioral economic principle to encourage or persuade or attract any consumers to increase consumption.

What is behavioral life-cycle model? This model explains consumer behavior can be persuaded to buy any discounted products by advertisement, e.g. television, radio, newspapers, magazine etc. promotion channels. Because frequent advertisement promotion method can let any consumers often remember the product's brand, discounted price, style, color and image from advertisement content.

So, advertisement can be one part of consumer behavioral life-cycle. For example, when the television audiences often watch TV. Hence, when the brand of product advertisement often makes fun image and discounted message to let TV audiences to remember this brand of product, when they are watching TV. Then, it has possible to persuade any potential consumers to choose to buy this brand of any products or consume this brand of any services, due to its advertisement of discounted sale message is very attractive to every one to let this advertisement audience's attention to remember this brand of products or services are selling or serving in market at this moment. So, it is advertisement image behavior influences audiences to buy the brand's any products attractively and persuasively.

3. Raising electricity consumption from electricity user individual habit

For electricity use market case example, how to analyze people's behavior in consuming electricity using a behavioral economic framework ? Electricity consumption is modeled by the means of consumer's individual useful habit, electricity price, consumer satisfaction level, willingness to invest in new technologies, social interactions, and marketing strategies by the power utility. Because electricity is necessary to every home or electric vehicle users needs or businessmen office etc. different needs every day.

Power companies supply electricity to a region's homes and industries. However, electricity needs modernization of power system companies expect to increase price. Due to competitive factor, such as other fuel resource choices, outdated kind of energy electricity supply, and renewable fuel energy source competition.

Hence, applying behavioral economic concept, I assume electricity consumers will compare to electricity and other kinds of energy choices to weigh up the costs and benefits of all alternatives, aiming to maximize their benefits, before making a decision to choose to use electricity for their house electricity demand or electric vehicle or shop or factory manufacturing etc. function of different aspects of electricity users.

For example, electricity business clients, they aim to reduce cost, such as energy expenditure, when they use any energy to manufacture their products in factories. If they feel electricity is expensive price to compare other kinds of energy power supply. When, they feel that they can not earn much beneficial advantages to use electricity to produce their products. Otherwise, if they feel other any kinds of energy supply can replace electricity to give more benefits to compare electricity energy. Then, many business electricity users will change to use other kinds of energies to consume to replace electricity power.

However, electricity can have competitive ability in electric vehicles market, if many drivers feel environment protection is more important to compare vehicles will be popular to be driven, due to many drivers don't want air pollution. They will like gas vehicles. Hence, the main attribute from the consumer side is one their habit electricity consumption behaviors, satisfaction level, energy efficient interaction with the power utility.

Consequently how to predict electricity consumer's demand. The important factor is how to let electricity users to feel power companies are changing a reasonable level to compare other similar energy supply products. When electricity users feel electricity which can bring more benefits to compare other kinds of energy products. Then, in energy supply market, if the demanding number of electricity consumers can increase more than other kinds of energy demanding number. Then, it is right time to raise electricity price to charge electricity consumers. Hence, how to persuade electricity consumers to feel that they can have more benefits to compare other kinds of energy products. It is the main successful factor to electricity power supply companies.

● Consumer confidence is as a predictor of consumption spending

Behavioral economists believe it has link between confidence and economic decisions to cause consumers to choose spending, if the consumer has confidence to believe the product is worth to use, then who will accept to buy the product to use.

Concentrated on the conceptualization of confidence and its role in mode in theories of consumption. It also concerns on whether the confidence indicators contain any information beyond economic fundamentals. The concern is whether confidence can be explained by current and past value of variables, such as income, unemployment, inflation or consumption or in other way.

Whether confidence measures have any statistical significance in predicting economic outcomes once information from the above variables is used. Economic variable factor will also influence consumer confidence to decide consumption spending, e.g. real consumption expenditures (income, wealth or interest rate).

Finally, it will identify under which circumstances confidence indicates can be a good predictor of household consumption. Hence, survey is one good measurement method to predict whether how much every household has confidence to spend to consume the brand of products to use. Why is survey a good confidence consumption measurement prediction to every household in every country?

The reasons include survey can gather every household consumption habit history data to evaluate whether every survey person has how much confidence to consume the brand of products. Which in most cases correspond to periods where there are large changes in household survey indicators, liking during financial crises or geopolitical tensions to measure or predict whether the country's future good or bad economic condition factor will influence every household consumption desire in the year.

This modelling approach assumes that there is a certain (unknown) in confidence index changes beyond which confidence starts impacting consumption behaviors. So, sample household surveys can show the contribution of confidence in explaining consumption expenditures increases when household survey indicators feature large changes. So that confidence indicators can have some increasing predictive power during the survey investigation period in the year.

Other view point, surveys have been concerned on whether the confidence indicators contain any information beyond economic fundaments. The concern is whether confidence can be explained by current and past values of variables, such as income, unemployment, inflation or consumption or the other way. Whether confidence measures have any statistical significance in predicting economic outcomes once information from different external variable factors to influence the survey household group.

What is confidence in consumption survey ?

Confidence in consumption. For example, to measure whether how much degree of strong inflation in the economy, such as recessions and recoveries will influence the country's household confident consumption in the year. The surveys consumers' questions usually concern on major expenditures and changes in the respondent's financial situation, focus on job availability and current business conditions etc. questions. It is then possible that about consumer confidence depending on the relative performance of the variables that may be more relevant balances, with respect to the factors that determine unemployment and other labor market related issues. It aims to investigate whether those any one of variable factors will influence consumers general loss confident consumption desire in this year.

What is a confidence indicator ?

A confidence indicator is considered as an explanatory variable for consumption together with standard variables used on predicting consumption expenditure. However, the natural real personal consumption expenditure is unexpected and unpredicted easily.

In conclusion, consumption expenditure depends the consumer individual confidence. If the consumer has much confidence to feel this year economic change will be better and he/she is easily to find job, then he/she will accept consumption easily in this year. It seems financial wealth and unemployment etc. economic factors will influence every household consumption desire. So, survey is one kind of good psychological consumption prediction method to predict consumption spending for any country in the year. I recommend manufacturers may choose to apply survey method to attempt to enquire sample survey people to gather data to predict whether what degree of consumption desire to them and find solution methods to solve low degree of consumption desire challenge.

How to apply behavioral economy methods to influence employee individual psychology to achieve raise productivity of long term incentive intention?

Increasing salary is short term incentive productivity method. Behavioral economy assumes labors will choose to do beneficial behaviors to themselves when they feel their work behaviors can earn more benefits to themselves more than their employers in the organizations. Otherwise, if they feel their work behaviors can earn more benefits to their employers more than themselves. Then, they won't choose to do their work behaviors, e.g. raising productivities or work hard. Due to they feel work hard or raise productivities behaviors that only give more benefits to their employers more themselves.

Whether does cheap product price incentive consumption desire to influence effective consumption behavior? Whether is monetary increasing salary payment incentive labors might be willing to work on task? I feel raising labors productivities is similar to raise incentive consumption, which both have similar point, such as increasing salary payment or cheap product price is the main factor to influence incentive consumption or raising productivities. Hence, it seems monetary factor is not the main effort to encourage labors to work hard.

In labor's behavioral economic view point, for example, if an employer pays an employee more doing a task, who might be less willing to work on it, who might be less productive given whose efforts and who may enjoy the task less. If you want your employees to save more for retirement. You may want to give them fewer investment options. If you want them to engage more in a task, you might want offer them an additional alternative, instead of increasing salary to that task. Thus, increasing salary is not only method to encourage productivities of incentives.

How to improve the design of incentive structures to encourage productivities in any organizations?

Any monetary incentive can only encourage productivities in short term. It can not only encourage productivities in long term in any organizations. It is similar to cheap or discount product price can only attractive consumers to buy the product in short term, it can not attract consumers to choose to buy the product in long term, it prefers to have more options to encourage labors to incentive productivities, e.g. investing good beneficial retirement plans. Suggesting that employees do not have free disposal of their investment options. These standard incentives seem irrelevant raising salary monetary factor, they can be quite effective in inducing labors to take particular actions to incentive productivities in long term. Due to when they can hard work, then they have more beneficial retirement plans or investing plans for their retirement. It means when they can achieve the most effective or efficient productivities to the employer for long term. It will give better retirement benefits and investment benefits to the better or even the best performance of employees. Otherwise, the worst performance employees won't earn good retirement benefits and investment benefits, when their employers feel their perform very poor in the organizations in long term.

Hence, increasing salary level method is not one successful long term incentive method to persuade every employee to raise productivities or encourage excellent performance optional method. Increasing salary level is only similar to reduce product price and it is only short term encouragement to consumption or productivities method.

In conclusion, extrinsic monetary factor can not incentive labor's raising productivities more than every employee themselves intrinsic motivation to raise productivities as excellent performance in any organizations. Thus, organizations need to let employees to feel that they can give long term economic benefits to encourage their intrinsic motivation effort to be raised their productivities or performance more effective or efficient in order to achieve long term both win-win economic benefits to employees and employers both.

Building employees and managers kindly co-operational relationship method

If you are an economist, your employer has no without any financial incentive to encourage your economic research tasks in your organization. It is equally difficult to certify that such activity will contribute to your growth of human capital and increased productivity in research or teaching. The standard model, which explains employee's effort only through the way (determined by productivity), is therefore incomplete. In particular, it doesn't consider that incentives to work do not have to be monetary in other words, that there are other things besides the disutility of labor (Kamenica, 2012) and section 1.3 have.

Why will short term wage increasing method only influence short term labor supply to raise productivities? The effect of reference raising wage can be most easily identified on short term labor supply to raise productivities. For US, New York city taxi drivers case, they have to decide every day for low long they are going to offer their services, given the day-to-day variable ability of demand they face (peaking during bad weather and/or when big conferences and public events are taking place in the city).

In the standard model, houses worked should grow with any growth in demand for New York taxi drivers' services. (one day's earning will have only a negligible income effect in the longer run). And yet actual cabbies work less on a demand heavy day. One of possible explanations suggests that New York city taxi drivers expect a certain income, they have set themselves a specific target income, who expect to achieve every day. During low demand for their taxi services, then they work longer hours to reach the target, when during peak demand, their referential income is achieved quickly and they only work short hours. Elasticity of hours worked with respect to their earnings is therefore negative (Lamerer, Babcock, Loewenstein, & Thaler, 1997).

However, taxi driver is either one self employment business or one taxi company employment driving service occupation. It is similar to other kinds of service jobs in societies. Servicing employees, such as waiters, salespeople, securities, customer services, bus drivers etc. different kinds of service occupations. They are not similar to manufacturing occupation to be applied how many amount of piece of products production to evaluate their productivities efforts. Thus these any one of service job nature is depended on their service performance to clients to feel their service performances are excellent to compare general service performance effort of service employees.

Considerably, respectively, I assume that if these service employees' managers can build kindly working environment, e.g. manager individual attitude and behavior can let their employees to feel happy to work together in their teams. Then, the managers' kindly as enthusiastic behaviors or attitudes will let every employee more positive encouragement of service attitude to serve their clients in their teams. Then, the client complaining number will be possible reduced, even none of any complains. Hence, building kindly relationship between managers and employees will raise excellent service performance to any organization service nature employees.

Can bonus method encourage service performance to be raised ?

In service job nature of bonus method can also raise employees' overall productivities or service performance. For example, when employees got a provisional bonus before the start of the workweek, but were warned that they would lose it on payday, unless they achieve the productivities or excellent service performance norm, they worked more productivities or let many clients to satisfy their service performance. Hence, managers can achieve bonus plan to compensate any excellent productivity or excellent services to them. Then, they can let clients to feel their service performance more satisfactory than employees of a control group who were merely given the standard promise to receive a bonus upon achieving the norm.

The effort was relatively small, however, productivity grew 1%. Interestingly, the effect of a loss was stronger when how teams were rewarded this way, social pressure came to bear on the less productivity team members. When the team members won't earn any bonus. So, long-term productivity gains were achieved through bonuses paid by excellent performance compensation method to compare to low service performance employees receiving no bonuses at all.

Economic views of human motivation nature

There are only two main types of economic actors and by making simplifying assumptions about how these types of actors behave and interact. The two basic sets of actors in this model are firms, which are assumed in this model are firms, which are assumed to maximize their profits from producing and selling products and services, households, which are assumed to maximize their utility (or satisfaction) from consuming products and services.

It seems any employees will choose to do behaviors to achieve to earn much benefits from their organizations. The models of economic behaviors that consider considerate employees' choice of goals, the actions they take to achieve these goals and the limitations and influences that affect their choices and actions.

For university students choose which universities to study case, suppose that any college enrollment students are deciding which courses to study. Thus, it implies that if the university can provide many different kinds of suitable or right courses to any college enrollment students to choose to study. It means that if the university can provide many different kinds of courses to enrollment students to choose to study. Then, it will have much chance to attract enrollment students to choose this university to study. It's competition can be raised by many courses choice factor. but, in fact, it is not absolute right, although the university can provide many courses to provide to enrollment students to choose to study. But, it is not guarantee to represent it must attract many students to enroll this university to study.

For example, suppose that college enrollment students are deciding which courses to choose to study. Although, it has right course to prepare to these enrollment students to choose to study. But, they see a summary of evaluations from hundreds of other students indicating that a certain course is very good in this university. Then, suppose that they match a video interview of just one student to give a negative review of this university of the course. Even when students were told in advance that such a negative review was worse to this university of the course. They tended to be more influenced by the negative review than the summary of hundreds of evaluations, even although such behavior seems irrational. Hence, although many right courses choice has much chance to attract students to enroll this university to study. But, if its bad educational quality from this course from negative review factor, which will influence the enrollment students number to be reduced.

It implies that students will compare this university's the course educational quality whether is better or worse to compare other universities' similar course educational quality, even this university's this course fee whether is reasonable in educational market. This is cost and beneficial comparison behavioral economy principle to all enrollment students before they decide to choose which universities.

Hence, this case implies that universities how to train teachers' teaching skills to let students to feel that they can learn new knowledge from their teaching staffs absolutely. It means how to raise education training skills to raise teachers' teaching performance. It is very important factor to influence the university's teaching development success. So, many courses choice is not important factor to attract many students to enroll the university. Otherwise, although the university can not provide many courses to let students to enroll, but it's teachers can provide excellent teaching service to teach whose students. This is important factor to attract many students to choose to enroll this university to study.

Under-level productive efficiency and low-consumption desire behavioral economic influences

In behavioral economic influence view point, I feel that under-level productive efficiency is the represent low production number to the manufacturer as well as low-consumption desire is not represent less consumers demands or customers lose confidence to the product.

On the one hand, I shall apply behavioral economic method to analyze why under productive efficiency is not represent low production number influence. Otherwise, I feel under-productive efficiency will have possible to increase production number after the manufacturer can review what factor(s) to influence under-productive efficiency.

I shall give reasons to explain as below:

As Jim, P. & Brendan. M. (2013) indicated who had ever been experiencing failure to do their businesses. Although, they had lost a million dollars, but they felt that they can be taught to learn undiscovered knowledge to know how to do their businesses successful by their wrong judgement and decision learning experience. They explained that " in ll risk taking, speculation, business ventures, entrepreneurial activities, it is the loss side on which you must focus first. This is even true for gambling, the gambler determines how much he's willing to bet, and loss, before the game is played. He doesn't wait for the game to end and then let the croupier or dealer assign his wager for him. How do you determine the downside, and how do you control or minimize it? With objective decision making and a plan that has as its starting point the stop-loss parameters"

Hence, it explains any business will have under-level productive efficiencies and low consumption desire business risk. However, to any one entrepreneur, who needs to know it is one game between the himself/herself and whose clients. They also need to know with objective decision making and a plan that has as its starting point.

Hence, I assume that if the entrepreneur has wrong decision to cause under-level productive efficiency, it is possible that, due to there is no enough employee number to manufacture the product or many employees are not skillful to manufacture all product in normal time or many employees are lazy etc. different factors to cause under-level productivities. However, when they discover their productivities are very low to compare similar competitors their employees' productivities and efficiencies. Then, they can attempt to find what factor(s) to cause low productivities and low efficiencies. it is possible that any one among of these factors case. They include many employees' lazy to influence low productivities or there is no enough employee number or many employees are not skillful to manufacture their products in production process.

Hence, wrong decision or plan is not represent failure. Otherwise, it can give chance to let the entrepreneur to learn whether what the factor(s) is (are) to cause low productivities and low efficiencies in whose product manufacturing process. As I feel that under-level productive efficiency is not represent low production number. Because I assume that if one worker lacks enough skills and manufacturing experiences to manufacture the product, but who can spend less time to manufacture the product and whose spending manufacturing time is same to the another owning enough skillful worker's time to do the product. Hence, I believe that the product quality from the low-skillful worker's manufacturing skill, it's quality will be worse to compare to the product quality from the high skillful worker's manufacturing skill. Hence, if the low skillful worker needs to spend much time to produce the product, but the product quality can be same to the high skillful worker's product quality. It means that it is sure because the low skillful worker has no excellent skill to compare to the high skillful worker to produce the product. Hence, his manufacturing spending time must be longer than the high skillful worker's time. It implies that the low skillful worker spends less time to raises high production number, but his product must be poor quality to sell. Then, his fast and efficient manufacturing speed that is not achieve economic beneficial to the organization's manufacturing process, e.g. less electricity spends to manufacture the product. Otherwise, the low skillful worker's fast and efficient manufacturing speed of behavior will raise the organization's cost in manufacturing process because consumers would not like to choose to buy any low quality product when they can choose which similar products to compare which one has the best quality and cheap price to buy.

Hence, efficient production is not the main factor to influence the business's success. Otherwise, good quality of the product factor is more important to compare it to influence the business's success.

On the other hand, I shall apply behavioral economic theory to analyze why low-consumption desire is not represent consumer demand lose to the business. As Jim. P. & Brendan. M. (2013) also identified " rather than looking for success to follow, who explained the formula for failure to avoid. As an Wang, founder of Wang laboratories said " it is my belief that there are no secret to success." The formula for failure is not lack of knowledge, brains, skills or hard work and it's not lack of luck, it's personalizing losses, especially of preceded by a string of wins or profits. It's refusing to acknowledge and accept the reality of a loss when it starts to occur because to so so would reflect negatively on you."

Thus, as whose feeling to explain why low-consumption desire is not represent less consumers demands or customers lose confidence to the product. The reasons include the causes of low-consumption desire are possible due to worse economic environment factor influences consumption desire to be reduced. It is not due to whether the product price is too high or quality is worse to compare others. Hence, as Jim & Brendan indicated the formula for business failure is not lack of knowledge, brains, skills or hard work and it's not lack of luck. It's not lack of luck. It's personalizing losses, means its reflecting to knowledge and accept the reality of a loss when it starts to occur. As it is applied to explain why low-consumption desire is not represent less consumers demands or customers lose confidence to the product. It's possible that external economic environment changing worse factor to cause the business personalizing losses, it is not reflect who lacks knowledge, skill, hard work factors to cause failure. Hence, ho to predict when and how and why economic environment changes worse will be important factor to predict when and how and why consumption behavioral changes to cause business's success.

● Demand and supply theory solves organizational problems

Any organizations can let salespeople feel happy to sell their products. Then their sale performance will also raise. The question concerns that how to make them to feel happy to help the organization to sell their products? I shall explain some methods as below:

How to manage sales for predictable revenue? In order to hold salespeople sale psychology whether they feel happy or unhappy, executives need to understand the essential activities, sales managers must focus on to be analysts for change, foster continuous improvement and create a sales culture that drives results. Sale executives need to know how to achieve top objectives of sales management is to drive sales, capture new revenue and exceed monthly sales and margin objectives, e.g. performing sale straregy development with each salesperson on Monday morning at a minimum, and in a formal one-on-one meeting during the week;using strategy tools and questioning techniques to ensure the prospects are qualified and the strategy is valid; knowing the ratio between future values and future monthly quotos to raise sale opportunities; six month on-going sale plan aims to make sure there are coordinated to achieve sale to various market segments; developing on ongoing series of networking events to build market awareness in order to ensure all salespeople attend specific events involved in networking by salespeople to, understanding the market how to influence salespeople sale method to sale number, understanding trends and seeking some channels to raise additional sales opportunities; how to create trained or warm sale environment to let sales teams feel happy to sell.

How to design and utilize efficient control sale procedures? The sale cycle procedure may include these market activities, such as advertising, sales promotion, market research, physical distribution, pricing , sale place, sale staffs seeking. SO, any organizations need have good sale planning, direction and control of the personnel, selling activities of a business with including recruiting, selecting, training, rating, supervising, paying or reward system, motivating strategy , as all these tasks apply to the personnel sales-force.

The factors may influence salespeople psychology, they may include fair income reward system, or appreciation methods and sale career development plan to every salesperson. It aims to encourage them to achieve the highest sale effort. Anymore, methods to train sale managers have the right direction to guide, lead and motivate their salespeople, e.g.

knowledge of salespeople psychology needs how to satisfy them, understanding why they choose to do or act themselves sale behaviors in order to improve their weakness to motivate salespeople to achieve company's sale target goal every month easily, e.g. raising profitability, sales volume, market share, growth and corporate image building raise clients' confidence to choose to buy this company's any products more easily.

The sales organization is required for the following purposes, they may include: enabling top-management, to devote to more time in policy making for the growth and expansion of business to divide and fix authority among the subordinates , so that they may shirk work, to avoid repetition of duties and functions, so that there may not be any confusion among them to locate responsibility of each and every employee , so that they can complete the whole work in stipulated time, if not then the particular person must be responsible, to establish the sales effort to enforce proper supervision of sales force.

What does the concept of salespeople replacement value mean? What is a sales force turnover management tool? Sales force turnover is defined as the rate at which salespeople leave an organizations, resignations, retirements or dismissals. So, if the organization can raise the sales force turnover ratio, because many salespeople can be promoted or the retirement, or the sales force turnover ratio raising reasons as well as they are not resignation or dismissal reasons. I believe that the organization ought have good sale environment and reasonable reward and welfare strategy to let its salespeople feel happy to help this company to sell its products every day.

However, sales management's actions have direct or indirect effects to impact on turnover. Direct effects may include the firm's firing or dismiss policy. The indirect effects on sale turnover may include new salesperon recruiting and selecting policies affect the quality and performance of the sale force as well as the speed at which salespeople are replaced. The same policies have an impact on the sales force turnover rate through the characteristics of the newly recurited salespersons and the promotion , training, retraining policies, support, supervision, compensation. ALl of those factors have an impact on salesperson's personal satisfaction or dissatisfaction absolutely. So, any sale organizations need to concern how and why whether any one of above these factors may influence their salespeople how to perform or act sale behaviors in order to excite their sale number more effective in long term.

How to achieve sale force management effectively? Sale management is one strategy to many organizations, because organizations expect their salespeople can only raise product sale number. So , they will consider whetther how to implement the sale management strategy to be the most suitable to themselves sale organizations in order to excite their sale teams to sell their products to achieve sale growth aim effectively. So for organization's long term sale growth development, it seems that one excellent sale management strategy can help the organization has stable sale number growth in long term possible.

However, the term " selling" includes a variety of sales situations and activities. For example, those sales positions where the sales representative is required primarily to deliver the product to the customer on a regular or periodic basis. The emphasis is this type of sales activity is very different to the sales position where the sales representative is dealing with sales of capital equipment to industrial purchasers. IN additions some sales representatives deal only in export markets whereas others sell direct to customers in their homes. So, sale organizations need to sell to local or overseas market as well as its target customer is businessmen or individual consumer or both in order to implement to choose their most suitable sale management strategy to train their salespeople more effective or achieving sale growth objective only. Because these its sale major target and where sale market place both factors will influence how it ought train its salespeople, so any organization's training method ought be influenced to change by whom is its major sale target and where is its major sale market location factors.

How to know the psychology of salesmanship? WHen the organization can predict or find reasons to explain why its salespeople feel unhappy to help
this organization to sell its products. Then, it can attempt to improve its weaknesses in order to let its salespeople to feel more sale service satisfactory feeling to continue to help this organization to sell its products. THen, it won't need not often to train or recruit new salespeople to replace its old salespeople in consequence. How to know what its salespeoples' real need in order to raise their sale service satisfactory feeling ?

Psychology means that " science of the mind" and psychology plays to important part in business and it is quite worth to bring to influence any organization salespeoples' posivitive or negative sale emotion in their every sale process between themselves and their every client in personal. For example, if the salesperson often have negative emotion or he feels unhappy in every sale process, then he will encounter or increase many times of sale failure possibilities. He will feel that he is one poor verbal advertiser or seller or promotor to help his organization to promote its products to sell again as well as he will lose confidence to sell any products next sale chance, because his failure sale experiences are accumulated to influence his sale emotion to be poor or difficult sale.

Hence, the poor performance salesperson needs have more successful sale experiences to compensate his / her prior many sale failure times feeling, if the organization hopes this poor performance salesperson can raise sale number easily. Overall, any organizations need to concern how to improve or raise the more failure times of sale experience salespeoples' sale techniques or methods or attitudes more than choose to fire or dismiss them as well as finding another new salesperson to replace him/her. Because it is possible that the salesperson 's poor sale performance that is not due to himself/herself poor sale effort and sale knowledge or lacking sale experience to the product, it may be due to the poor sale team cooperation relationship , feeling poor or not comfortable sale physcial shop environment, poor sale manager and other salespeople working relationship, the sale manager lacks leadership effort, poor family relationship etc. external factors more than himself/herself personal poor or negative emotion or poor health etc. personal factors. Hence, the organization ought enquire him/her why he/she feels unhappy to sell its products and it needs to attempt to find methods to solve his/her challenges immediately. If his/her challenges can be solved. It is possible that his/her sale efforts can be also raised for. So, if the organization can know how to utilize positive sale emotion psychological methods to predict or know why and how every salesperson perform his/her sale behavior in whose daily sale tasks, then it can concentrate on implementing effective and the most suitable sale training to raise their sale abilities more easily.

However, the sale training may include: How to build or improve long term good salesperson and his/her customer sale service relationship between every salesperson and every client in every buying and selling cycle process, how to using right communicating styleds for better understanding every client's real needs, powers and negotiating, e.g. every salesperson needs to review why there are many clients do not choose to buy any products from his sale presentation or promotion, finding every time sale failure reasons can let the salesperson makes himself/herself sale failure reasons evaluation or judgement in order to find what is the major reason influences his/her sale failure, e.g. lacking product knowledge, he/she often let many clients to feel that he lacks patience to listen the client's enquiry or feedback, his sale presentation is not attractive to let many clients like to stay longer time to listen his sale presentation in whole sale process, the salesperson himself/herself emotion is negative and he /she can let many clients feel he / she is not happy or does not enjoy to sell this product from himself/herself face impression or sale behavior impression easily, lacking enough sale techniques to persuade his/her clients why he/she ought choose to buy this product in whole sale process etc. these factors may influence the salesperson's sale failure chance to be raised. Hence sales manager ought need to spend long time to meet the poor sale performance salesperson to discuess what his/her sale challenges are the most major to influence his/her every sale successful chance in order to improve his/ her sale performance more successfully.

IN conclusion, the reasons why salespeople often encounter sale failure possibilities. The factors may include these aspects, such as they lask the desire to help customers to make satisfactory purchase decisons, they only concern how to achieve sale final objective or aim only, it will cause clients feel they do not real concern their real needs. They only concern to sell the product in success. They do not know how to describe the product whether what characteristics or features it owns accurately in order to increase sale chance to persudade them to make final decision to by the product, they do not attempt to participate the whole sale process to help them to choose the most right product in order to satisfy their any purcahse needs, they ought avoid deceptive or manipulative influence tactics, avoid the use of high pressure sales techniques etc. Thus, if any organizations can spend time to investigate what factors cause why any one of salespeople choose perform his/her sale behavior often in order to know or understand their salespeople' sale psychology absolutely. Then, I believe that their sale number will only grown more easily.

CHAPTER TWO

Sport industry entertainment consumer pscyhology

Nowadays, the sports business industry is made up of establishments and the employees of corporations who are primarily concerned with aspects of sports having to do with management, marketing, economics, and finance, amongst other venues. The sports business industry focuses on the sports themselves, as well as the place of sports in society, and the principles that support the sporting industry. The sports business industry is involved in the merger between sports and business, and how these fields work interactively for mutual benefits and profitability.

The sports business industry is interdisciplinary and may involved planning sporting events and effectively marketing for sports, as well as working with accounting, communications, law, and psychology skills. The sports business industry tackles the development of risk management plans for any legal issues that may occur, the negotiations of contracts for players in the industry, and/or strategies for effective media relations.

In fact, instead of sport indutry may include any kinds of sports, e.g. swimming, football, basketball, table tennis, tennis, riding bicycle, climbing, running etc. different kinds of sports to let young and old people enjoy lives. When they play any kinds of sports, they must need to spend some money to any any kinds of sport tools, e.g. swimming pool, table tennis hand tools, bicycle , football, basketball etc. sport useful tools. So, if any one kinds of sport industry can develop in good suitation, then it can influence the sport related useful products sale number because when the sport entertainment player chooses to spend time to play the kind of sport, then the kind of sport sports need be influenced to rise needs. So, if the kind of sport is popular, then the kind of sport product will also influenced to rise needs. So, how to develop the kind of sport in order to attract global sport entertainment players to choose to play the kind of sport, this sport development factor will influence the kind of sport need or innovative development and its related sport products useful tool need increases globally.

● How legalization impacts sports betting economics

A closer look at factors shaping the future of online sports . For example, Americans place $50 billion to $60 billion a year in illegal sports bets, dwarfing the legal $5 billion in Nevada sports betting. This represents a potentially enormous market now that states can decide whether to legalize sports gambling. Although exciting, uncertainties remain that will impact industry size, scale, and opportunity moving forward.The current state of sports gambling. In the immediate US the Supreme Court's decision to overturn the Professional and Amateur Sports Protection Act (PASPA) in May 2018, some states scrambled to pursue a lucrative opportunity independently, without a federal framework in place. Delaware and New Jersey, the plaintiff of the Supreme Court Case (Murphy vs. NCAA), were the first to act and have seen major returns, with more than $385 million a month being wagered in New Jersey alone. Eight states have currently legalized sports gambling, with more to potentially follow in short order as bills are reviewed by state legislatures. These near-term developments will be interesting to watch as sportsbooks lobby for legalization on the state level.The federal government is attempting to secure a wider blanket agreement on the federal level to protect public welfare and the integrity of the game, and generate sufficient tax revenue. The leagues support a federal framework because it can address their interests on a national level. The sportsbooks would prefer legislation that mirrors the way gambling is currently regulated on the state level by the Nevada State Gaming Commission. This situation, like many legalization efforts, is extremely fluid and will change rapidly as the critical uncertainties mentioned below unfold. Depending on the outcome, companies that are able to get in on sports betting could realize a substantial payout.

Hence, global sport entertainment poduct merchants or suppliers, they must need to know how to avoid the illegal sport products can be sold from internet or online channel to enter the kind of sport product market to compete to them illegally any time. Due to ecommerce is popular , so it influences many sport entertainment products consumers may choose to buy any kinds of sport products from online in preference. So, they can not neglect these illegal sport entertainment product sellers' sale behaviors from internet any time.

For US sport industry development example, economists estimate the economic scope of the sports industry in the United States. Drawing on a variety of data sources, they investigate the economic size of sport participation, sports viewing, and the supply and demand side of the sports market in the United States. Estimates of the size of the sports industry based on aggregate demand and aggregate supply range from $44 to $73 billion in 2005. In addition, participation in sports and the opportunity time cost of attending sporting events are important, but hard to value, components of the industry

Sport is a complex, multi-faceted activity encompassing modern spectacles like the Summer and Winter Olympic games and informal pick-up games on urban basketball courts; a recreational jogger, a runner in the Boston Marathon – a competition with thousands of participants -- and people watching the Boston Marathon on television all participate in sport in some way. So, such as Boston Marathon sport game example, if it can provide good sport entertainement show to let global sport auidence to feel exciting and visable enjoyment. Then, the year Boston Marathon competitive game can help advertisement industry and the tennis sport product industry increase tennis products buyer number and advertisement entertainment income and the Boston Marathon competitive game show income. So, one good sport competitive show may help the country's GDP growth, e.g. World Cup football competitive show, World Cup riding competitive show, World Cup swimming show etc. So, any countries government can not neglect how to develop and innovate and promote themselves any sport competive shows and sport entertainments in order to raise GDP growth and create more related sport occupations to reduce unemployment ratio in our nowadays society.

Relatively little attention has been paid in the past to estimating the economic scope of the sports industry, perhaps because of difficulties formulating an appropriate economic definition of sport. A sizable literature documenting the economic scope and economic impact of specific sports or sporting events, already exists, in part because of the ease of defining the limits of events like a golf tournament or season of professional baseball sport industry.

One key issue in defining sport involves identifying criteria that separate sport from games of skill like chess or poker and from recreational activities like dancing, hiking, fishing, and gardening. A secondary issue involves identifying criteria that appropriately define competition in a way to distinguish sport from exercise. For example, running has a competitive dimension but jogging does not. Note that weightlifting is an Olympic sport, bodybuilding is a professional sport, and competitions based on athletic performance on fitness equipment like stationary rowing machines, elliptical trainers and stationary bicycles exist, blurring the already murky distinction between exercise and sport.

In estimating the economic scope of the sports industry is to define the industry in economic terms. Several frameworks for defining the sports industry have been proposed; much of this research emerged from Europe, where government policymakers took an interest in estimating the overall economic importance of sport several decades ago. While a national income and product accounting approach has some appeal, because of the well-developed methodology and the existence of rich set of frequently updated accounts for many developed economies, it also has some weaknesses. First, on the national product side the analyst is at the mercy of the existing production classification system. All levels of government are involved in the provision of sports facilities and other important activities on the supply side of the sports market, and national income and product accounts do not contain detailed estimates of government spending on many specific items. Much of the activity in the sports market involves non-traded goods and labor inputs not valued at market prices, such as WORLD CUP SPORT COMPETITIVE GAME, WORLD GOLF, WOLRD TENNIS SHOW as well as any sport service workers they are needed to work in these any one big shows. Hence, the sport show audience number will influence any one these sport show income and employees number. The sport show employees needing number will depend on these activities factors , such as:

1. Activities involving participation in sport

2. Activities involving attendance at spectator sporting events

3. Activities involving following spectator sporting events through some media.

We recognize that each component contains elements that could be defined as recreation, exercise, or games of skill. For example, including participation in sport means that some activities that could be defined as exercise, like aerobics or walking, will be included in our definition. Including spectator sports means that auto racing, figure skating, and other such activities will be included in our definition.

Individuals can participate in the sport market in three ways: by participating some sport, by attending a sporting event, or by watching or listening to a sporting event on television, radio, or the internet. Each generates direct and indirect economic activity. All three take time, and economic theory tells us that time use has an opportunity cost. In this case, the opportunity cost of individual participation in sport is the value of the next best opportunity for an individual. For consumers of sport, this opportunity cost can be valued in terms of forgone wages or earnings. Furthermore, participating in sport requires equipment, fees, and potentially travel, all of which generate economic activity. Attending a sporting event involves purchasing tickets, travel and perhaps other purchases like food and souvenirs. Watching or listening to sporting events requires equipment, in the form of televisions, radios or computers, as well as subscriptions to broadcast services. Since all of these economic activities increase with the number of participants, documenting the number of participants is an important indicator of the scope of the sports market.

On conclusion, more importantly, individuals' participation in the sports market generates significant economic benefits beyond direct and indirect economic activity. Individuals derive satisfaction, or utility, from participation in the sports market, which has economic value. In economics view, individuals' participation in the sports market produces consumption benefits. These consumption benefits are not bought and sold like tickets, but they are important when assessing the overall scope of the sports market. Although placing a dollar value on sport related consumption benefits is beyond the scope of this paper, it is safe to say that the value of these consumption benefits rises with the number of participants in the sports market.

● Sport consumer behaviors

Despite the recent rapid spread of leisure involvement and loyalty research, very little attention has been given to the conceptualization of the nature of involvement's relationship with loyalty of sport fans. Whether psychological commitment and attitudinal loyalty intervene in the relationship between sport fans' involvement and their behavioral loyalty to a soccer team. For a soccer team sport competition example, it indicate that psychological commitment and attitudinal loyalty intervene in the relationship between sport fans' involvement and their behavioral loyalty to the soccer teams. It is suggested that marketing strategies may be developed to strengthen psychological commitment and attitudinal loyalty in order to maximize behavioral loyalty.

Involvement has been defined as 'a person's perceived relevance of the object based on inherent needs, values, and interests' (Zaichkowsky, 1985, p. 342). Leisure involvement refers to an unobservable state of motivation, arousal or interest toward a recreational activity or associated product that is evoked by a particular or stimulus that possesses drive properties (Iwasaki & Havitz, 1998).

So, any sport competitive show's audience , their psychological commitment factors are very important. They may include: psychological commitment ,attitudinal loyalty behavioral loyalty. For example, psychological commitment is a mediating variable between involvement and behavioral loyalty. Additionally, attitudinal loyalty is a mediating factor that facilitates the relationship between psychological commitment and behavioral loyalty. It seems that not all highly involved spectators become loyal to their team, although higher levels of enduring involvement seem to be an important precursor to behavioral loyalty. Higher levels of psychological commitment, in which attitudinal loyalty is a crucial element, appear essential for the development of spectators' behavioral loyalty to a team. The development of spectators' behavioral loyalty appears to be best explained as a progressive process in which the formation of high involvement seems to be a precondition for becoming a committed spectator of a team.

On conclusion, any sport competitive shows, how the show can influence and attract audience, the entertainment attractive factor will influence the time sport show success in sport industry long term development. So, how to develop sport entertainment show, it will be one important issue to bring any country's sport income nowadays.

● SPORT HEALTH INFLUENCES SPORT CONSUMERS NUMBER INCREASES

I beleive that when one country is experiencing stable economic growth, it will lead more healthier, I shall indicate reasons as below:

How can economic growth lead healthier to poor people? Can economic growth influence medical service quality and doctors and nurses medical service performance of hospitals? Can economic growth influence quality of medicine to let patients to eat in order to raise more healthier? Has economic growth and medical health service (production of medicine quality) direct or indirect relationship to lead patients more healthier? What are health impact income?

I assume that life expectancy will be better, if the country has better economic growth or it improves its economic growth. I shall indicate the reasons include as below:

Firstly on relationship hand , I believe that it has relationship between income and health or life expectancy hand, due to the country can develop or grow up or grow its economy to remain long term good economic development. So, its citizen can have more jobs supply to do to treat any sickness. So, they will have effort to buy different kinds of medicine to eat in order to raise more healthier. It seems that some economists support long term good economic growth will bring the country's medical development, e.g. many hospitals can have more effort money to spend to research any new kinds of medicines to let patients to choose the most health medicines to eat, when patietns have different kinds of medicines to choose to eat in order to choose to eat th enough nutrition improvement of different kinds of medicines. Then, the country's patients will have more chance to treat their sickness to be improved health.

Hence, it seems that hospitals will have enough money to research ,when the country has long term better economic growth condition. When the country can remain long term better environment growth improvement, it can lead many jobs to be supplied to people to work and they will have more income to save to buy any expensive medicines, if they are facing serious sickenss, e.g. cancer. Then, they can buy this cancer medicines to eat to treat cancer disease (non common sickness) in order to be more healthier.

Thus, economic growth can lead medical industry has enough money to carry on researching any new kinds of medicines to attempt to treat any serious diseases in order to provide different kinds of new medicines to human to eat to treat any serious diseases more healthier. For example, U.S., U.K. these both developed countries can remain long term good economic groth. So, these both countries have enough money to assist domestic hospitals to carry on researching any new kinds of medicines to let patients to choose the most effective or more healthier medicines to let patients eat to attempt to treat their serious diseases more successfully. So, U.S., U.K. serious diseases of patients whose death ratio is decreasing in these two countries as well as their death ratio, due to serious diseases causing is the least to compare to other countries.

Secondly, I shall indicate on the improvement in health and economic growth hand, how any why it has relationship between improvement of human health and economic health. I shall focus in particular on the question of how much of the improvement in health can be attributed. The improvements in the health can include that human's living of standard, better nutrition, changes in the public health environment, it includes sanitation and supply of clean water. Finally an improvement in medical technology, for example, both sanitation improvements and treatment with antibiotics will reduce mortality from infectious diseases.

However, we can explain why economic growth and improvements of human's health , which has relationship. It can be measured by mortality, it can be linked to specific changes in both ages at which people, i.e. an increase age of the number of patients to disease, such as U.S. , U.K. these both countries, the number of old age people who have serious diseases of the total population ratio is less than the developing countries, e.g. China, Africa. It is possible to explain because these both countries have stable long term better economic growth to compare these both developing countries.

Thirdly, I shall indicate on the better nutrition of food supply and economic growth relationship hand. It seems that better economic growth in the country , it will encourage the country people have more consumption effort, then they have enough food to earn more better nutrition to live. So, their diseases will be reduced, due to they have enough food to supply to them to eat to earn more nutrition from different kinds of foods every day, e.g. beef, pork meat, vegetable , fruit etc. food. Hence, economic growth can encourage any food consumers have effort to spend too much expenditure to buy any kinds of fresh and good taste and better nutrition of food to eat. So, it implies the long term stable economic growth will encourage human to buy any kinds of better nutrition of food to eat every day. It can lead human has better healthier, due to human can hace more money to buy better nutrition of food to eat. It includes the special poor people who have effort to buy better nutriction of food to eat.

To sum up, the better nutrition of food is mainly to be consumed by the more effort of the country' poor people when the country have good economic growth environment. So, economic growth can lead any countries' hospitals to research more different kinds of medicines to be attempted to provide to any serious diseases patients to eat. The country's poor people can be raised more healthier to live in the stable economic growth countries.

● Sport industry development brings economic growth

   I believe that economic growth must have relationship to influence human development. But it must not lead positive human development.

Otherwise, when one country is experiencing stable economic growth in long term. It is possible to lead negative human development. I shall indicate as below:

To explain whether economy growth can influence human development. We need to research whether economy growth has relationship to influence human development. What is economic growth meaning? Economists explain it means an increase in gross national product (GNP) if all products and services that an economy produces during a specified time period. So, it brings one interesting question concerns economic growth: IS it a quantity based concept, not quality based concept? If economic growth is an only relationship to economic development Otherwise, if it also has quality based concepts, then it has relationship to influence or lead human development. When economy growth is a direct measure of changes in the size of the economy. Whether it is a measure of welfare to human development or sustainable development.

Why do we need to concern economic growth? Because political importance means domestic and international trading income and the country's people earning income measurement as well as humanitarian importance means an indicator of welfare, an indicator of human development and an indicator of sustainable development measurement. However, if seems GNP or GDP measures that value of products and services produces within an economy (economic income) in a given year, but it can also measure of welfare development, sustainable anything. Otherwise, human development includes welfare, which measures quality of life and human development, which means quality based concept as well as sustainable income, which means how much we can spend without running down capital stocks, we can maintain same level of spending in perpetuity. Hence, human development concerns our quality of life or standard of living. So, human welfare separation of means from a direct measure of well-being as well as economic welfare separation of means GNP or GDP corrected for expenditures on various necessities. So, it brings this question: Can GDP (economic growth measurement) be an indicator of human development or human welfare? I shall indicate cases to attempt to explain as below:

For GDP per capita and happiness case example, I assume that the country , US increases rapidly up to capita US $4,000 per capita in this year and small returns after that. What does this mean? What influences US people feel happy or happiness feeling causes? For another changing in

GDP correlate to changes in environment quality case. Environmental KC (Kuznets Curve) showed the graphical representation of Kuznets theory from the 1940 year that economic inequality increases over time, then at a critical point begins to decrease. Environmental KC (EKC) shows a hypothesized relationship between various indicators of environmental degradation and income per capita.

The EKC (environment Kuznets Curve), shows that in the early stages of economic growth degradation and pollution increase, when beyond some level of income per capita , which varies for different indicators. The trend reverses , so that at high-income levels economic growth leads to environment improvement. This implies that the environment impact is an inverted u-sharped function of income per capita. Thus, EKC implies that economic growth has relationship to influence or lead environmental pollution causing, due to many factories are manufacturing any products during economic growth period. All air or water pollution will increase, due to factories manufacturers manufacture lot of products. The scale effort brings that economic growth increases environmental pollution if there is no change in other factors. The other factors include that change in output mix, change in input mix, state of technology, production efficiency and demand for " improved environment". Hence, when these factors have no change and factories need to use many resources to manufacture lot of products in the manufacturing process. It will bring serious pollution, due to these factories have not improved its technology, production efficiency to avoid to pollute environment to cause local pollutants, deforestation, biodiversity, river low quality, carbon and air low quality, waste increases with increased income. Hence, it is an evidence to explain economic growth will have possible to cause pollution indirectly as well as poor quality of life (standard of living) to influence our life. IT is a good evidence to explain how economic growth can lead human's quality of life (standard of living) to be poor. SO, it brings these questions as below:

Should we always aim to increase GDP? Should we choose to either gain ultimate happiness or either increasing GDP? Is it an indicator of wealth to depend on what GDP really measures? Should we need to concern environment degradation cost or our nervous stress from environmental pollution causing?

In conclusion, it implies that economic growth can lead positive human development , such as economic welfare influence, but it can also lead negative human welfare of long term air or water pollution influence and this challenge can not be solved to any countries in our life if any countries do not attempt to keep balance between achieving economic growth and clean environment in order to not influence our quality of life to be poor. The important evidence , it explain it has relationship between economic growth and human development and they have cause and effect relationship.

● Economic growth leads human
employment growth

I believe that when one developed cuntry is experiencing stable economic growth, it can lead human employment growth in high technologic job market, but it can also bring unemployment to low knowledge or skill job, such as cleaning, laboring job market, due to artificial intelligence technology will replace many low skillful job in the future. I shall explain as below:

I assume that it has positive relationship between the accumulation of human capital relation to total employment and GDP growth. It means that a positive relationship between economic growth and the demand for qualified labor are consistent with the hypotheses of the form in the industrial export sector positively influenced by the accumulation of human capital. I shall explain the reason why economic growth can lead positive human employment growth as below:

Namik, (1965) explained that economic growth theories reflect on the continuous increases in the gross national product, because of interaction that occurs in a given environment; in a certain time period, including various changes in the presentation of productive factors in society labor, capital and nature resources to lead these radical changes to increase successive demand on commodities and hence an increase in national income.

Hence, society labor knowledge or skillful development will be one important factor to influence any country's economic growth. If the country has many good educational and skillful labor, then the country will have more possible to raise economic growth for long term, due to they can apply their expertise skills and knowledge to attribute to their country's different kinds of high skillful or knowledge jobs or occupations to do in order to raise themselves country's productivities efficiently. Hence, economic growth has more effort to raise human (labor) these knowledge or skillful development in possible. Considering how economic growth leads labor's skillful and knowledge development positively, I shall indicate these factors as below:

Firstly, on manufacturing industry labors development factor hand, I assume that China's industrial export sector has been positively influenced by the accumulation of human capital , due to many China young people who had graduated any different kinds of degrees, e.g. engineering, education, law, accounting, business, management, chemical , medical , architectural , biology, medicine, computer science, earth science, space science, ocean science, environmental science etc. different kinds of subjects from overseas universities or local universities. Them they apply their expertise knowledge to attribute their skills to do any kinds of professional jobs in China's society. Due to China's sudden economic growth , so it reflects on the continuous increase in the good gross national product, because it occurs in a given good economic environment in a certain time period, due to the global different kinds of China's product number need is increasing as well as many China product manufacturers need many high educational and skillful labors to attribute their effort to help them to develop their businesses in China during the good economic growth period. Hence, China's economic growth leads China's any kinds of product manufacturers who need to employ any kinds of high educational and skillful employees (labors) to do their different kinds of jobs , due to global any kinds of China product consumers' needs are increasing suddenly. Then, it causes the effort to China employees who prefer to spend expenditure to train any young graduated people to be qualified high educational skillful labors with the good conditions of production; which leads to competitive sectors to attract these lacking working experiences of young graduated people t to be the availability of qualified labors in China in order to raise enough employment supply number to satisfy China's manufacturers' labor needs. So, it is a reason to explain that China's high educational and skillful labors development aims to attract foreign investment at a time. The overseas countries seek to provide investment environment through international laws and regulated that only provide qualified labor able to deal with modern technology to China's manufacturing industry development. So, China's economic growth will lead China's knowledge and skillful labors development in possible.

Secondly, on human capital education accumulation factor hand, economic growth will lead human capital educational level to be raised. I shall explain that why economic growth can lead human capital education accumulation positive reason as below:

I shall suppose that the negative impacts in the economic growth rate, it will bring the poor qualified human capital education level. I believe that it has direct relationship between education and the economic growth rate. I shall also suppose that the principle variable of interest determining GDP per capita is the level of labor supply which accounts for all the different educational level, (i.e. primary education, secondary education and university education).

Human capital accumulation can be explained to contribute to utility maximization. In general, it is a direct contribution in the utility function, this is because the more human capital each individual can accumulate in terms of knowledge and skills, the more happiness will be obtained for each one. Hence, it brings this question: Why can economic growth lead human capital accumulation educational level to be raised? The reason is because that when one country has good economic growth, then any primary, secondary and university schools have enough effort or resource to raise teacher individual teaching skills in order to teach many high knowledge and skillful level of students and satisfy their learning needs. Hence, the factors of these primary, secondary and university schools' educational inputs will also be raised, such as the teacher individual characteristics, their educational quality and educational experiences and qualities of their educational services provided and the interest of the country in accumulating educational high level of human capital need. For example, when the country encounters a high economic growth rate, it is able to demand new technology ,as a result of its well-educated society , such as China is one developing country, it needs a well-educated society to educate or train its high educational or skillful labors when it is experiencing in one good economic growth period. So, China's firms encouraged to adopt the advanced technologies developed in high income countries , when global economic growth is coming. It will cause the country, such as China will need to educate many high educational and skillful level labors to do any kinds of high technological jobs in itself country. So, China is a developing country because it needs to develop high technological manufacturing industry, it explains how its economic growth leads high educational and skillful labors development.

Consequently, such as these two cases indicate that one country's economic growth will be possible to lead high educational and skillful labors development in order to raise its competitive ability in different kinds of industries. In specially, high technological development industry , it needs significant high number of educational and skillful labors to satisfy the country's labor market when it is experiencing good economic growth period because many country's high technological product industry is their main income source. So, when the these countries are experiencing good economic growth period, it will lead the human employment growth positive effect for this kind of industry in possible.

● Economic growth leads income
inequality

I believe that when one country is experiencing stable economic growth, it will bring serious negative influence to raise income inequality bewteen high education and low education people's income. I shall explain the reasons as below:

Why does the country's economic growth lead negative income inequality influence? Does either the country's high economic growth lead high income inequality or its low economic growth lead low income inequality in appropriate rate? I shall explain that what reasons to lead income inequality, when the country has high or low economic growth influence as below:

Many economists believed that the relationship of reverse causation from inequality to growth. It has a negative relationship between high economic growth and income inequality. I assume that the gross domestic products per capita to the level of inequality in income distribution. The unequal distribution of income seems similarity to the economic development process.

In fact, the first time , the economic development tends to increase inequality, but the trend is reversed, inequality stabilizes, the decrease until it reaches the lowest level that can be seen in the industrialized economies. So, when the country is encountering farming or agricultural economies or this farming industry won't be easier to lead income inequality. Such as Africa is a farming industry African income level won't have significant income inequality, due to it lacks high technological economic development in itself country and its main jobs are most relate to farming, low technological and low educational need of different kinds of farming jobs. So, the high income and low income people's salaries are not significant difference too much. Otherwise, industrialized economic country, such as China, many Chinese workers are working in different kinds of industrialized jobs in China. However, although, the industrial industry brings economic growth in China society. But, China's high and low income of industrialized workers' wages, they have large significant difference. For example, the computer programmers and computer inventor salaries and the computer manufacturing workers' salaries, they have large significant difference, for another example, the vehicle designer and vehicle inventor salaries and vehicle manufacturing workers' salaries, they have large significant difference. Due to computer programmer or computer inventor needs have high technical knowledge, but computer manufacturing needs have low technical knowledge as well as vehicle designer or vehicle inventor needs have high vehicle components knowledge to invent any kinds of new styles of vehicles, so their salaries must have high income significant difference to compare the vehicle or computer manufacturing worker. Hence, due to their educational and skillful level is significant difference, so it causes their income will have much significant difference in industrialized industry.

Hence, although China is encountering economic growth, but it also leads high income inequality to China's labors, due to it is one industrialized country. For Africa farming country example, its main industry is agricultural sector, designed as the traditional low-productivity sector in the Africa economy and it can not be replaced easily by the industrial sector. In this traditional farming industry, Africa can not develop its economy to grow up easily. So, it leads its labors' salaries level , which has less or low income inequality causes. Otherwise, such as China is a industrialized industry country, it has different kinds of industrialized development of this sector, such as the computer manufacturing or computer program sector and the vehicle manufacturing and vehicle design invention sector, which produces a movement of labor form low-productivity to high productivity sector, e.g. the vehicle sector is one low number productivity sector and computer sector is one high number productivity sector. This is reflected by an increase in income inequality in China's industrialized society.

Hence, such as above cases, Africa is one farming country, so it causes economic growth is slow and African income level is less inequality. Otherwise, China is one industrialized country, so it causes economic growth is fact and Chinese's income level is more inequality. It can conclude that fast economic growth country will lead high income inequality.

Otherwise, slow economic growth country will lead low income inequality. Banerjee and Newman (1993) indicated a relationship between the choice of occupation and the development process with the presence of an imperfect credit market. In this context, the occupation requiring a high level of investment is undoubtedly devoted to the wealthiest of the population. So, they believed that and industrialized countries will have more occupation choice to let themselves country's people to choose the best salary level of jobs to work. Due to industrialized development causes their economic growth is fact. So, it causes many occupations are created to let themselves country's workers to choose to work, then fast economic growth causes many occupations creating and it leads high income inequality. Otherwise , the farming countries, they have slow economic growth. So, it causes less occupations choice to let themselves people to choose to work and the slow economic growth countries will lead low income inequality.

Consequently, it explains that it has relationship between whether the country is industrialized economy or farming economy or technological economy as well as high economic growth or low economic growth . Then, it has also relationship between high or low economic growth and more or less occupation choices. In final, it has relationship between more or less occupation choices and high and low income inequality. In sum up, high or low economic growth will lead high or low income inequality in possible.

Reference

Iwasaki, Y., & Havitz, M.E. (1998). A path analytic model of the relationship between involvement, psychological commitment and loyalty. Journal of Leisure Research, 19(2), 256-280.

Zaichkowsky, J.L. (1985). Measuring the involvement construct. Journal of Consumer Research, 12(3), 341-352.

CHAPTER THREE

Tourism and the entertainment age:thought on an international travel phenomenon

Nowadays, tourism entertainment activity is very popular. Every country government must have itself tourism development strategy to seek how to persuade other countries' tourists choose to travel to its country in preference. So, tourism entertainment incomce will be one imporant market share to any countries' overall GDP income. How to excite other countries tourists to choose itself country to travel in preference. It is one interesting question to any countries' tourism policy decision market. I shall indicate some cases concern how to predict and excite travellers' entertainment psychology in order to bring attractive tourism experience to any countries as below:

THE USE OF SOCIAL MEDIA AND ITS IMPACTS ON TRAVELLER BEHAVIOUR

Nowadays, internet is popular to use. Social media enjoy a phenomenal success in terms of adoption and usage levels. They cause every day lives on how people connect and communicate with each other, on how they express and share ideas, and even on how they engage with products, brands, and organizations.Moreover, social media became significant networks of consumer knowledge. In travel and tourism, the impacts of social media have already been described as tremendous, primarily due to the experiential nature of tourism products, and especially of holiday trips: purchases are considered risky and therefore decision making processes are information intensive.

Moreover, social media is all about facilitating people to express and share ideas, thoughts, and opinions with others. It is also about enabling people to connect with others, like they were doing for the last thousands of years. However, what is of significance is that social media: (a) removed spatial and time constrains that were inherent in traditional methods of communications; (b) provided online tools that enable one to many sharing of multimedia content; and (c) employ easy to use interfaces that enable even non-specialists to share and connect. So, any travellers plan to go to anywhere to travel, they will apply internet to attempt to seek any countries' hotel price, air ticket price data as well as seek any countries' destination whether it has anywhere places or locations, they are worth to visit before they decide to go to the country to travel, even they will seek whether the country anywhere have any restaurants to provide the good taste food to them to eat, choosing which kinds of public transportation tools are the most cheapest or the fastest to arrive the destination to travel.

The travellers they will feel to make the accurate expenditure budget before they decide to go to the country to travel when they apply internet to seek any travelling data. Even , some travellers will apply internet media to discuss to other travellers by email media communication channel conveniently.

For example, facebook is the most popular social media

networing. During the last years social media are enjoying a phenomenal success: Facebook, a social networking website, many travellers like apply this facebook social media channel to discuss and share their travelling experience together. So, any travellers can apply faccebook social media to know whether

the country's any destinations , anywhere are worth to visit or not. Hence, if one traveller had planned to choose the country's some places to travel, but when he feel negative emotion when he discuss with another

traveller concerns his past travelling experience to his travelling planning destinaton. Then, he will be influenced to change another country's travelling destination to travel. Hence, facebook media brings the sudden and rapid travelling plan change to every travellers when they discuss their travelling experience

in their online travelling discuss process.Thus, online social media can bring these several aspects of influences to any gathering data online travellers. They may include as below:

It is one kind social media use and impact during the entire holiday travel process as well as throughout the holiday travel related consumer decision making processes. It influences during which stages of the holiday travel process to any travellers feel that they need to gather any travelling data from social media before they decide to travel any destination in habit. Hence, online social media can bring impact active users' travel related consumer behaviour in popular.

According to The World Wide Web Consortium (W3C 2004), the web has numerous impacts in society and culture, science, industry and business: In society and culture the web provides a new medium of worldwide human communication and revolutionized access to information and knowledge with implications in all aspects of the daily life from religion and sex to health, politics and commerce. In science, the web has drastically changed the way scientists are doing research: It enables real time access to an enormous amount of information via sophisticated but user-friendly search tools, facilitates cooperation between scientific communities, serves as a new platform for conducting primary research but also as a channel for the dissemination of scientific knowledge. Due to the web, consumer preferences and the decision making process are not influenced only by the traditionally defined controllable and uncontrollable stimuli. They are also influenced by the "web experience", or the "online atmospherics" consisting of online controllable factors such as website usability, interactivity, trust, aesthetics, online marketing mix (Constantinides 2004), and by the website's quality, interface, satisfaction and experience (Darley et al. 2010).

On the other hand, there are also signs of negative implications: The Internet and the web makes consumers highly individualistic, more time driven and demanding, more information intensive,
dictating timing and mode of communication, and with increased expectations (Akehurst 2009).

In addition, the vast amount of information available on the web causes an information overload, impacting negatively on the ability of users to locate information relevant to their needs (Radosevich 1997). Thus, it seems that word wide web or internet invention which can influence travellers feel negative emotion very easy when they apply facebook social media to discuss themselves past travelling experiences. If some travellers often share their negative
travelling experiences to other from facebook social media, when the other

travellers read their negative travelling feeling from the words and they will write down on paper to remember
the travelling destinations are not value to attempt to travel.

Then, there are many travelling places are not very attractive to let many travellers to feel when they often share their negative travelling experiences from facebook social media. Although, some travellers want to find the best or the high value of travelling destinations to travel, they shall attempt to discuss or enquire any travellers' opinions from facebook social media. But, in fact, there are many travellers want to find the worst or the less value of travelling destinations from facebook discussion. Hence, facebook social media can influence many travellers' to change their prior destination choices to another later desitnation choices often, when they get the negative travelling experience to share together from the social media internet channel any time.

● Tourism industry element

The tourism industry relies a lot on services and operations; we can classify the operating sector into different hospitality, they may include: accommodation sector, trade trade sector,event sector,attractive sector,entertainment sector, adventure and recreation sector,tourism, transport sector and food sector. Each of the sectors above is different in the services it renders, but sometimes they rely on each other to be more efficient.

The entertainment sector which is the main focus of the research could also be categorized into different segments.These any one service sepect must be important elements to influence overall tourism income and they have close relationship. For example, when one traveller feel the hotel can provide comfortable feeling to satisfy their lving need in his short trip time as well as he can find any entertainment activities easily as well as he can find any cheap and fast public transportation to catch in his trip any time as well as he can find any restaurants to eat good taste food in his whole travelling trip when he visits this country first time. Then, all of these enjoyment and comfortable of travelling feeling will influence he remember this country is one valuable travelling place and he also feels that he ought continue to choose this country to travel again and again. So, if the country can provide the overall travelling activities to satisfy any traveller individual living, eating, transporting and entertainment need. Then, its tourism industry will develop rapidly. For example, theme Parks aims to create an atmosphere of another place and time, and usually concentrates on one dominant theme, around which architecture, landscaping, costumed personnel who are sometimes known as animators, and different facilities for entertainment, distraction, recreation, or physical activities, such as rides, shows, food service and merchandise, are coordinate, because the different facilities in a theme park belong to the same enterprise. (Weiermair,& Mathies, 2007, 228.) Examples are the Walt Disney Magic Kingdom, Disneyland, Sea World Florida, Europe Park Universal Studios and many more. Theme parks are majorly child-friendly, which makes them interesting places for families to visit and they are usually filled with numerous exciting rides, a carnival atmosphere, and several cartoon and movie characters.

On conclusion if any country hopes to develop itself tourism entertainment industry in success , one country needs to consider many different aspects of entertainment facilities to let travellers to feel fun, excite and comfortable and enjoyable in order to let them can not forget this travelling entertainment activity choice in his/her live. Because any travelling related service elements will have important influence to every first time traveller individual psychology, if the country's any travelling related services can provide the positive emotion to let every traveller to feel. Then, the repeating travellers number will have more chance to increase because they still feel this country can provide the best travelling entertainment service to let them to feel to compare other countries in their life.

● Traveling entertainment industry leads urban
environmental planning development need

I beleive that when one country is experiencing stable economic growth, it must lead urban environmental planning development need, I shall indicate reasons as beow:

Can one country's long term stable economic growth lead urban environmental planning development to itself country? Do they have direct or indirect cause and effect relationship between them? I shall indicate some causes to explain whether they have cause and effect relationship between of them existed.

Mexico city is one good example to explain whether itself economic growth has relationship to lead itseld urban environmental planning development recently. Nowadays, Mexico city's economic growth is stable, so it has effort to develop a more livable interlinkage of economic social, and good environmental city to provide to Mexico people to live. It has been developing more livable city by building an efficient intra-urban bus system, expanding urban green space, and meeting the basic needs of the urban poor. Hence, it implies that when one country has long term stable economic growth effort, it is possible that it will plan to develop it's urban environment in order to let its people to live more comfortable, such as Mexico city recent urban environmental planning development core example. So, it explain that why economic growth will bring human's living needs to gain satisfaction in possible.

However, I bring one question: Does it has possible to develop the urban environmental development to achieve the most effective and beneficial to the country's cities , when it had been experiencing the long term stable economic growth period? I shall indiate some evidences to explain this issue whether it can be possible to occur as below:

Every country has thousands of possible sustainable cities, for each city has unique historical , cultural, political and environmental circumstances. Such as U.S. , U.K. these both countries, which have many cities, e.g. Washington, New York, London etc. cities. Every city has unique cultural, historical , political and environmental circumstances backgrounds. So, their urban environmental planning needed to be adapt from approaches formulated in cities and regions, where problems of infrastructure, social equity, and urbanization of the environment have been creatively addresses. They need to know how to design every city's urban to impact on the environment more adapt to make cities more livable for human.

In fact, in economic view point, due to our earth has limited natural resources will continue to provide life support for humanity's lives. So, every country needs to know how to use our earth's limited natural to use our earth's limited natural resources to develop every city's urban environment to let every city's people to live more comfortable to avoid the lacking enough earth's natural resources to be supplied to them to design urban environmental function for every city use in the future one day. Because every country's cities; human population tends to grow, but every country's cities' lands area supply is limited. So, it will cause every city's natural resource is not enough to supply to human to use, when the city's human population growing number has exceeded the city' land area supply to suppot the city's human normal population to live. Hence, it is a value considering question: How to use our earth's natural resource effectively and efficiently and organizing, e.g. land area. It can avoid future natural resource, such as land supply shortage causes human can not satisfy comfortable living environmental need in every cities.

Traditionally, economists have been concerned with the efficiency of resource use. They have been slow in developing economic models that adequately account for resource scarcity and pollution. Only rarely have economists worried that some resources may be short supply, such as clean land and soil , clean water, clear air and theat if these resources are used indiscriminately, they may become exhausted for every city population growth need for which, the city's urban environmental is needed to plan and develop. So, human expected to have comfortable lifestyles.

We need to know how to choose to do our behaviors to avoid environmental pollution, e.g. land, air, water qualities dirty pollution, when the country has long term stable economic growth, it can not neglect how to avoid environmental pollution to every city as the same time. So, when one country has long term stable economic growth. It also needs to plan how to reduce land, air, water natural resources are used by human's wrong attitudes or behaviors to use our earth's natural resources. So, it implies that when one country has long term stable economic growth, it also needs to consider how to plan to develop its urban environment efficiently and effectively and organizing in order to satisfy every city's people's comfortable living needs.

Hence, I bring this question: How to keep stable economic growth and enough natural resources supply to urban environmental development to different countries' cities? I recommend that when every country government needs to encourage businessmen consider environment protection issue when they choose to do and kinds of businesses in themselves countries.

Keating, (1993) explained that how to utilize local materials and are energy-efficient, non-polluting and labor intensive as well as every country government needs to achieve action progress of energy conservation and renewable energy, such as wind, solar, hydro-electric renewable energy, and biomass. For transport policies that favor public, bicycle, and food transport over automobiles municipal development designed to reduce commuting and land use that contains urban sprawl and prevents it from encroaching upon agriculturall land and environmentally sensitive areas are enunciated.

To sum up, in human development history, our earth was relatively empt of human beings and our belongings are only include (man-made capital) and relatively full of other species and our habitats (natural capital). In ago human development history, because human had no any business economic activites. So, human does not need to expand much natural resources to do any business economic activities. Hence, human had enough natural resource to be supplied to use. Till to nowadays, years of economic growth have changed that basic owning enough natural resource supply pattern. As a result, the limiting factor on future encouraging growth has changes. If man-made and natural capital were good substitutes for one another, then natural capital could be totally replaced.

How the two are complementary or however , which means that the short supply of one imposes limits. I shall indicate fishing boats catching fishes to sale business example to explain the economic growth and natural resource shortage relationship issue. If one day, the country's ocean had enough fishing boats to catch fished to sell, but it has without enough population of fishes to be caught to let the fishing boats to catch to sell in the ocean. Once the number of fish sold at market was primarily limited by the number of boats that could be built and manned, not limited by the number of fish in the sea. This suitation is better, due to the natural resources of fishes supply number is enough in the sea. It is only the fish catching boats number is not built enough factor. This cas is similiar to urban environmental development to cities case. When the country had developed long term stable economic growth ,it needs to consider whether human's standard of living is raising up or falling down as the same time. Such as this fishing boats catching fishes business case. If human only consider whether the fishes catching number is increasing every day . But human neglect to consider that one ocean will be polluted and fished will be killed by pollutants. Then, the shortage of different kinds of good taste fishes number challange will cause. Although, human has enough woods or steels resources to build any kinds of fishing boats, but it can't solve fishes shortage challenge. Then, it will lead fishes supply number shortge and it can lead human's living of standard to b fallen down, due to human has no enough fishes to be supplied to eat because many fishes are killed by pollutants in sea. It is similiar to human's urban environmental planning development case. When, human only consider how to remain long term stable economic growth, e.g. building many houses in the limited land area cities, it will damage the city's land green plant and tree growth natural environment as well as the city product manufacturers neglect to avoid to pollute river, air and ocean in their factories manufacturing process. Then

, in long term time, when our natural environment is polluted. Any cities will have only polluted dirty air to human to breathe and dirty water to provide to human to drink and any cities lack enough green and clean soil to grow trees and plants to let human to live comfortable in different cities. Then, human's standard of living or quality of life will be fallen down. So, human ought consider economic growth will lead natural resources number to be decreased as well as environmental pollution challenge causes, due to human's economic action lead this challenge causes.

Consequently, economic growth has possible to lead urban environment planning development needs, due to human had polluted our natural environment and consume the exceed number of natural resource to cause any vegetable and fish and food supply number to be reduced in long term stable economic growth period to every country's economic development. To avoid human needs to reorganize cities and urban environmental development need. Huaman must need to find solutions to avoid to cause serious pollution to our land, sea and river and air in our long term stable economic growth period.

In conclusion, when one country is experiencing stable economic growth , it can perform better economic development. But, it can not absolute perform better human development. Due to human only considers how to do any business behavior to damage our natural environment and misuse our natural resource. Otherwise, when one country is not experiencing stable economic growth, it is possible to lead human development. Due to it's economic development stage is not reach the maximum period. So, the country won't do business behavior to damage its natural environment and misuse natural resource to cause itself people's standard of living to be worse.

reference

Akehurst, G., 2009. User generated content: the use of blogs for tourism organisations and
tourism consumers. Service Business, 3 (1), 51-61.

Constantinides, E., 2004. Influencing the online consumer's behavior: The web experience.
Internet Research, 14 (2), 111-126.

Darley, W. K., Blankson, C. and Luethge, D. J., 2010. Toward an integrated framework for
online consumer behavior and decision making process: A review.

Psychology &
Marketing, 27 (2), 94-116.

Radosevich, L., 1997. Fixing Web-site Usability. InfoWorld, 19 (50), 81-82.

Weierman K, Mathies C, 2007, The tourism and leisure industry, shaping the future, Binghamton, Haworth press

World Wide Web Consortium (W3C), 2004. W3C 10th Anniversary [online]. Cambridge, MA:
World Wide Web Consortium. Available from: http://www.w3.org/2004/Talks/w3c10-
Overview/ [Accessed 12 December 2009].

CHAPTER FOUR

The reader's reading method choice psychology

It is one interesting question to predict and measure why the reader chooses the book to study or how his /her reading habit behavior or
reading attitude which can influence her/his reading interest or reading book choice in this book sale market. I shall indicate some factors why and how influences reader individual reading behavior or book choice as below:

● Fair Pricing of The eBook or paperBook Perception Factor

Internet can influence buyer choice,such as whether the reader either choose to buy the ebook or paperbook choice .People will pay for convenience, entertainment, art, education, enlightenment, fun, the ability to have something instantly and many will even
pay a little more for a product that is friendly to the environment. In reading industry, ebooks are all of that and they can be read again and again
without costing readers more. People love to be entertained. They love to be enlightened. They love convenience. They love instant gratification.
So why is it that publishers are fighting a pricing battle for ebooks? For example, Amazon wants to see ebooks at $9.99 or less, publishers are fined for allegedly trying to price fix ebooks and readers demand to know why they should have to pay the same for an ebook as they do a paper book.
With authors, publishers, booksellers and consumers all trying to be heard on this topic of ebook prices the question persists; how much should ebooks cost?

In the economic "supply and demand" view, what cost to readers and to the publishing industry? Reading the flurry of articles written about
the DOJ's charges of price-fixing, as a reader, I initially felt like I was being taken advantage of. I must be, because the DOJ is forcing publishers to pay

back some of the money readers paid for books. So obviously readers were over-charged, right? Not necessarily. And I realize that the charges against the publishers are about the conspiracy and not a reflection of what the government thinks ebooks should cost.

Regardless of what it costs to create a book, if no one is willing to pay the price publishers are asking then one of two things will happen; either publishers will offer less books, taking less chances on new authors, or publishers will have to cut costs in other ways to lower pricing. Or, perhaps, publishing houses are no longer needed. So, ebook publishers can replace paperbook publishers more easily if ebook price can keep very low to compare any one paper book price. Of course, a lot of people are speculating to benefit from self-publishing or are struggling to be part of an industry that can't afford them.

When publishers cut costs in order to meet the demands of readers for less expensive books, then the publishers can't take chances on publishing books that are not a sure bet to make money, leaving many out of work authors to move to self-publishing, setting lower prices that publishers are then expected match, which causes them to make less money from epublish online sale channel.

What does this have to do with ebook pricing? A lot really, because it causes us to focus on the side effect of the problem instead of the problem itself. The problem is that no one is addressing the psychology of fair pricing of ebooks from the point of view of the end consumer; the reader.
Self-published authors are setting their own prices, often starting at $1.99. There are a lot of valid reasons to do this. The author may be looking to gain new readers by selling their back list, their previously published books in which the rights to the book have reverted back to the author, which is a good idea, or the author may just be looking to make money by selling high quantities of books. Some authors are new and keep the prices low knowing many readers are more likely to purchase a book from an author they are unfamiliar with if the price is low enough. But, big publishers and authors,who have been serially rejected by publishers over the last few years, and are happy to hear the message of antiquated publishers in New York frightened of the future and how those publishers will one day regret rejecting the author.He is also an influencer. Recall that his site did not display a button for books that cost more than $9.99.

On the other hand, readers see the $9.99-or-less message in many places on the internet. Amazon favors the $9.99 price even when it means they will take a loss selling at that price. They do that as a business strategy to put other booksellers at a disadvantage and in some cases to put them out of business. And though most everyone in the industry knows of this practice and what its intent is, the government chose to see publishers as price-fixing when Apple and several New York publishers got together to discuss how to combat the effects of Amazon's pricing tactics and try to figure out how to take back their right to publish books at the prices they feel is fair.

Hence paper book publishers will face competition from ebook publishers because their prices are often lower than their general prices when they are displayed on an book shops.

What is a fair price for an ebook? How is that determined? It is determined by a lot of factors.

How much does it cost to create the ebook? How much is a reader willing to pay?

The problem is that publishers have not done one aspect of their job correctly. Yes, publishers do a lot of great things and they do it very well, but the one thing they should have excelled at, the failed at, and they are now paying the price for it. They have done nothing to create a psychology of fair pricing within the reader that matches the price they want to get for a book.

Publishers should be working on campaigns that promote books in ways that people are made to understand that a price of $15 – $25 for an ebook is a fair price. They should promote books so that people don't second guess what a fair price is. Do publishers not recognize the issues readers have with ebook pricing? Are they so focused on Amazon that they don't see the needs of their customers? However, paper books still have its attraction ,such as they can be sold, such as second hand book, when the book original buyer does not want to read the book, then he can sell cheaper price more easily. Otherwise, ebook can not resell to anyone in success because they are only read from internet channel. So, if the paper book is more attractive on reading and its price is reasonable, then I believe that it can still attract many readers to choose to buy it to read from book shop because readers believe it can be sold more easily.

Some points to make about ebook prices compared to paper book prices-People tend to think that having an actual, physical book in their hands, one they can share, re-sell, put on their coffee table and mark on (yes people do mark in their books), are all reasons why they are paying a higher price for a book.

Those are all good reasons, too. We will infer, for the sake of this lengthy article, that people include "good story" and "known author" as part of their acceptance to paying more. The issue seems to be that people feel an ebook has less value because you can't do those things with it. That is simply not the case. In fact, it's not paper and harder to display on your coffee table and you can't re-sell it or even share it as easily as you can a physical book but you're paying for something of equal value in the trade-off. You don't have to cart around heavy books everywhere you go. You can have instant gratification because you can buy the book and start reading it immediately from the comfort of your own home.

It is friendly to the environment. It is convenient, given that many books are available across platforms including your computer,

mobile device and/or tablet as well as in some kind of cloud system. So if you forget your ereader at home, but have your mobile phone, you can still read your book.

On conclusion, there are things a reader can do with a physical, paper book that cannot be done with an ebook. There are things a reader can do with an ebook that cannot be done with a paper book. The reader is paying for preference. They are paying for what they want, how they want it. Where does that de-value ebooks in the mind of readers? That is the big question, isn't it? Because it is easy to access a book online readers sometimes think ease, less valuable. But that's not true at all.

Ebook reading will become one kind of reading habit from mobile or laptop when the reader leaves his home in any time. Most readers will pay extra for life to be made easier for them. That's why there's valet parking and beauty salons. Yes, we can do those things ourselves, but we pay a lot of money each year to have other people do those things for us. Why? Because it's easier on us. So, ebook reading can let readers go to anywhere to read from their mobile or laptop. It is one kind of attractive new technological reading or learning behavior nowadays.

On conclusion, ebook reading habit will be replaced to traditional paper book reading habit in possible. Perspective is hard to change, especially once someone takes the lead and begins to create expectations. It is up to the publishing industry as a whole to band together and change the perspective of the reader when it comes to ebook pricing.

Hence, if paper book publishers hope to win their ebook publishers, they need to charge the reasonable book market price, it can not rise highly to

compare its similar ebook topic, because when one ebook reader discover
one ebook price is very low to compare one paper book, they
have similar contents and topic , then he will prefer buy the similar topic
and content ebook to read as well as the paper book must need
to design photo to attract readers' reading interest and price is more
reasonable in the paper book sale market. When he read the paper book
long time, he feel bore to read, then he believe that he can sell this paper
book (seond hand book) to anyone in less discount price more easily.
When this both factors can achieve that the paper book will also be sold to
anyone more easily.

● Electronic Publishing industry brings
knowledge-based economic society

I believe that when one country is experiencing stable economic growth,
it can raise knowledge -based economic society, I shall indicate reasons as
below:
I shall explain why and how economic growth can raise the country to
become one knowledge-based economic society. Knowledge investment
means that knowledge distribution is through formal and informal
networks, which is essential to economic performance, knowledge -based
economies which are directly based on the production, distribution and use
of knowledge and information. Knowledge is increasingly being codified
and transmitted through computer an communications networks in the
information societ. For example, the developed countries, e.g. U.S., U.K.
. They have long term stable economic growth for may years. So, they
had been experiencing the knowledge-based economic developed social
coutries. Their knowledge-based economic societies will provide them the
enabling organizational change at the U.S., U.K. firm level to maximize
the benefits to them in both manufacturing and service technology for
producing sectors.
The effect of "knowledge"-based economy, which will led a fuller
recognition of the role of knowledge and technology in economic growth
(human technologial capital) growth to assist or encourage human
development. For example, the exports of high technology industries had
grown fastly for these knowledge of economic growth developed countries,
e.g. Canada, U.S. , U.K. , Australia, Japan, New Zealand, Europe etc.
developed countries.
Knowledge-based economic development can also lead more intangible
investments in research and development, training of the labor force,

computer software and technical expertise to those above countries. So, knowledge-based economic development can lead human's talent development to create new talent human's knowledge to different technological development aspects, e.g. internet invention, 3 D printer invention, advanced medical equipment invention, space boats, nuclear energy invention, prior speed railway transportation tool invention etc. technological products. So, any one of high technological products invention which must need have good economic growth to the country, then when the country has good economic growth condition,it will have effort to train or educate talent human to attribute to knowledge -based societies to encourage or give these chance to talent human or inventors to invent any kinds of high technological products for human to use. Hence, when one country can have effort to be developed to one knowledge-based economic developed country. Then, it can have possible to provide high technological resources to educate or train " talent" humans or scientific inventors to invent any new kinds of high technological products to provide to human to use. So, in the future, oue standard of living will be improved in possible, due to economic growth causes any kinds of high technological products to be invented to provide human to use.

However, I bring this question: Can economic growth bring knowledge-based economic society to lead talent human development really? I shall indicate reasons to explain whether they have relationship to lead talent human development as below:

When the country has good economic growth , employers need skilled labor number will increase in the highest demand. Although, the manufacturing sector is losing jobs, but employment is growing in high-technology, science-based sectors ranging from computers to pharmaceuticals, high knowledge-based jobs. These jobs are more highly skilled and pay higher wages than those in low technology sectors, e.g. textiles and food processing. Moreover, knowledge-based jobs in service sectors are also growing strongly. Indeed, non-production or knowledge-based job in service sectors engage in the output of physical products are the employees in most demand in a wide range of activities from computer technicians, through physical therapists to marketing specialists. The use of new technologies, which are the engine of long -term gains in productivity and employment. Generally improve the " skills base" of the labor force in both manufacturing and services. And it is largely balance of technology that employers now pay more for knowledge than for manual work. So, it seems that economic growth will have possible to cause knowledge-based economic society to any countries.

Then, I shall explain the question: Can knowledge-based economic society lead talent human development? In fact, it is not a new idea that knowledg plays an important role in the economy . Also economists are now developing new growth theories to explain the forces which drive long-term economic growth. In new growth theory, knowledge can raise the returns on invetment, which can contribute to the accumulation of knowledge. It is done by stimulating more efficient methods of production organization as well as new and improved products and services. Knowledge can also spill over from one firm or industry to another with new ideas used repeatedly at little extra cost. Such spillovers can ease the constraints placed on growth by scarcity of capital.

Hence, it seems knowledge-based economic society will encourage employers to train talent human to contribute their any new kinds of knowledge to do any kinds of new creating jobs. Moreover, knowledge-based economy can also encourage employers to create more different kinds of new knowledge jobs to lead talent human development.

The talent human development includes these complex-areas of knowledge in order to fulfil their jobs as below:

For example, practitioners of law and medicine belong to know-who , it refers to knowledge about " facts ". This knowledge is close to what is normally called information. Know-why refers to scientific knowledge of the principles and laws of nature. It means technological development and product and process advances in most industries, e.g. research laboratories and universities organizations. So, firms need to interact with these organizations either through recruiting scientifically -trained labor or directly through contracts and joint activities. Know-how refers to skills or the capability to do something. A new product or a personnel manger neede to select and train staff have to use their know-how.

One of the most important reasons for the formation of industrial networks is the need for firms to be able to share and combine elements of know-how. Finally, this is why know-who because increasingly important. Know-who involves information about who knows what and who knows how to do what. It is possible that any talent human expects he.she knows how to use whose knowledge efficiently. The know-who kind of knowledge is internal to the organization to a higher degree than any other kind of knowledges. It is significant in economics, skills are widely disposed because of a highly developed division of labor among organization and experts. For example, for a modern manager who must need to own this kind of knowledge to manage whose organization efficiently and effectively in order to achieve the most maximum beneficial to productivities and raising employee individual working performance.

In conclusion, it seems that it explains why the knowledge-based economic country's employers need to spend expenditure to train talent humans in order to raise their different aspects of knowledge development, when the country is experiencing " knowledge-based economic society".

CHAPTER FIVE

Software entertainment game consumer behavior

How information technologic game strategy influences game player entertainment psychology? How and why information technological game strategy can influence economic growth? I shall explain as below:

Nowadays, Macrosoft and Microcorp are the global information technological big companies. They own much market share in global information technological industry. Whether what factors influence they can still be global information technological products leaders. Why does computer software consumers still choose their products to compare other software products in preference? I suppose that Macrosoft and Microcorp, their hypothetical any software games have developed a clever new computer game that is certain to be very popular. Although Microcorp have the unique competitive advantage with its own software game engineers and compete against Macrosoft, but it can so it cheaper and better if it can hire any Macrosoft's software game engineers. So, in economic view, it needs to pay high salary (higher cost) to hire Macrosoft's engineers (labor), but Macrosoft's engineers can help Microcorp to invent any new kinds of software games to compete Macrosoft. Although, Microsorp needs to pay higher labor cost, but when it can raise its any software games' design and game playing methods to attract any game players. Then, these new and exciting software games can help it can bring many game entertainment players and then it can sell cheaper price to raise more attractive effort to win its competitor (Macrosoft). So, higher software game designing engineers (skill labor), their game designing effort will be the major factor to influence any one information technological companies in success. If one software designing company can employ one high software game designing effort profession to help it to design any kinds of attractive software games.

Although, it may pay high salary (labor cost), but it have much chance to attract many software game buyers to compare that if it pays less salary to employ one poor game software designing profession. Because the poor software game designing profession may need to spend long time to research how to design any kinds of attractive game software to excite game players' playing desires in this playing software game industry market. Long time research to the poor software game designer may be one none any reward to compensate to the software game designing firm when it needs to pay long time salary to employ him. Otherwise, if the software game designing firm can accept to pay higher salary to the higher software game designer, he will have higher chance to help it to design any more attractive software games to influence game players' playing game entertainment desires. So, any software game designing companies their game designers (labor) must be the major factor to influence their business succeeds or fails in this software game entertainment market.

On the employing method hand, Microcorp can choose to include in its contracts with its software engineers that from working for another Macrosoft software company for a certain period of time if they resign from Macrosoft. A move such as this is sometimes called a preeptive move. Its propose is to alter its rivals' payoffs in order to alter their employing strategies. Preemptive moves are usually costly (high slaary), and this one is no exception. In its employment contracts makes Macrosoft a less attractive to let its old game software engineers want to leave their current employer, such as Macrosoft. As a result, Macrosoft must pay its software game designing engineers above the going market salary if it hopes their employment contracts can be continue between Macrosoft and its software game engineers.

Should Macrosoft must need to decide how to react. It can choose to fight Microcorp by aggressively advertising its game, which is costly high, but gives it a larger market share in the game player entertainment market, when Macrosoft had any one profession game software engineer(s) leave(s) his company and he/they change(s) to the another Microcorp software game designing company to work, or it can forego the expense of an advertisement campaign and simply share the market 50/50 with its major competitor, Microcorp to be partners.

Their competition has close relationship to influence economic growth because it will have many game players number to be increase if they can cooperate to be partners in success when they can design any new kinds of software game products to satisfy software game players' entertainment feeling. Otherwise, if they can not be one good partners and they only consider their every business benefits and neglect themselves business benefits. Then, their software playing games sale price can either to be reduced in order to attract any software game players when their software games can not be designed to have much new playing methods to attract many game players. Consequently, the GDP income to this software game entertainment market must reduce because any kinds of entertainment software games prices are reduced as well as the game players number is also decreasing. Due to they are the major software entertainment game suppliers in global. Any game players will only choose either Microcorp or Macrosoft to buy their any kinds of entertainment software game products to play majorly. So, their software game manufacturing and sale number must influence global GDP income increases or decreases in macro economy view. It implies that any countries technological software game industry's GDP income will depend on these both Microcorp and Macrosoft software game's cooperation relationship whether they have good or bad cooperation relationship. If their cooperation relationship is good, then they can manufacture high quality and attractive entertainment software games as well as raising sale price and exciting many game players' entertainment desires to achieve the increase to game players number aim more easily.

How to achieve their cooperation relationship more easier. I suppose that, in the software game entertainment industry, over its lifetime, the computer game will generate $500,000 in new income (income minus production cost) for all the firms producing it or its clones. Macrosoft must pay its software engineers an additional $100,000 to get them to agree to accept a contract containing an anticompetition clause. It costs Microcorp $100,000 to develop the software if it can hire Macrosoft's engineers and $200,000 otherwise. Aggressive advertising costs Macrosoft $70,000 and has the effect of giving it a 80% market share if it restricts its engineers' employment and a 72% market share if it does not. So, the fall in total market share is caused by the fact that without some of Macrosoft's advertisements. If however, Macrosoft passively acquiesces to Microcorp's entry and shares the market, then both firms can still achieve a 50% market share fairly. Hence, they must need to achieve 50/50 market share if they hope to achieve the cooperation relationship in success. Otherwise, they will not achieve cooperation relationship in success.

However, the spending advertisement factor will also their cooperation chance in success. For example, it would be more realistic to recast the Software Game as one in which Macrosoft chooses how much to spend on advertising with sales depending continuously on the amount spent. Other examples of continuous cooperation choices may include: the productive capacity of an electrical power plant; the salary to offer a prospective employee; or the insurance premium to charge a prospective policyholder. So, the amount to any of these expenditure factor will influence whether they will decide to cooperate to sell their software games products in global game entertainment market.

How and why Macrosoft and Microcorp's cooperation can influence global economic growth? It is significant that Macrosoft and Microcorp both technological software game designing companies are global the largest firms, they are doing international software game trade business to many countries and they have large market share in the software entertainment game sale market. Aside from trade based on technological gaps and software game product cycles, software game entertainment industry is dynamic in nature or game players' entertainment taste will change any time in completely static in nature. That is, given the nation's game players' playing taste and game entertainment factor, such as game playing designing technological method and game player individual playing game taste both. We proceeded to determine the nation's comparative advantage and the gains from the different kinds of entertainment software game designing supply factor and the game player individual game taste changing factor. So, any nation's software game players number will depend on these both factors to influence whether their number will either increase or decrease in the year in this global software game entertainment market. However, these factors can be changed by time, technology usually can improve any software game playing methods and game player individual playing taste will also change any time. As a result, the nation's comparative advantage also changes over time, such as when the nation has many game players lose their interest to buy any software games to play, then the nation ought not only consider how to develop its software entertainment game in the technological industry, it is right time to research any other new technological industries to develop if it still hopes its GDP income can rise in the technological industry overall aspect. Such as dynamic trade theory is still in its infancy. However, our comparative statics analysis can carry us a long way in analyzing the effect on international trade resulting from changes in factor technology, and tastes over time, such as entertainment software game case.

The growth of factors of production will also influence the software game entertainment industry development, through time, a nation's population usually grows and with its size of its labor force , such as China and India. Similarly, by utilizing part of its resources to produce capital equipment, e.g. India needs to utilize its technological resources, technological engineers and technological material can need to be used to manufacture either new software game products or computers. But, its technological resources will be shortage (both labor and technological material). So, many technological companies choose to apply more technological material and technological engineers to use much time and money to manufacture any new software game products. Then, these labor and material resources will be reduced to be spent time and material to manufacture any new computer products in the year. In this technological industry case, capital refers to all the man-made means of production, such as machinery, factories, communication and education and training of labor force, all of which greatly enhance the nation's ability to produce either computer products or software game products. So, the national will also continue to assume that it can experiencing economic growth is producing two commodities, such as software game and computer both kinds of technological products under the constant returns to scale. So, if India can not raise the rapid technical process to skill labor and supply technological material supplying number to satisfy to manufacture the enough software game and computer products to supply them to sell to any countries' playing game players and computer users every month. Then, its technological industry will lose many clients, due to it can not supply enough software games and computers number to sell to any countries.

Several empirical studies have indicated that most the increase in real per capita income in technological industrial nations is due to technical progress and much less to capital accumulation. However, the analysis of technical progress is much more complex than the analysis of factor growth because there are several definitions and types of technical progress, and they can take place at different rates in the production of either or both commodities, such as software game and computer.

Technical progress is usually classified into neutral, labor saving , or capital saving. All technical progress , regardless of its types reduces the amount of both labor and capital required to produce any given level of output. So, if India could have good technical progress to raise its technological labor skill and reducing the technological material to be used to manufacture the software games and computers. Then, it will have chance to keep the maximum manufacturing level number to software game and computer products as the same time.

On conclusion, it is only Macrosoft and Microcorp's cooperation relationship can influence their any kinds of entertainment game products' playing qualities and entertainment taste to let game players feel more fun and exciting beacase when these both big high technological entertainment game designers like to attempt to cooperate to manufacture their any new kinds of entertainment game products to let children or young people to play in order to satisfy their exciting and actual enjoyment entertainment feeling when they can feel to be the actual person to participate to any game image environment influentically. Because their cooperation relationship can improve their game paying qualities and raise entertainment enjoyment performance more easily than the their competive relationship in this entertainment game market.

● SOFT GAME market consumer behaviors

Future when the thinking capabilities of computers approach our own is quickly coming into view. Raid process in coming decades will bring about machines with human –level intelligence capable of speech and reasoning, with a myriad of contributions to economics, politics and warcraft. The birth of true artificial intelligence will profoundly affect humankind's future. In our future technological development market, what it will bring much influences to economy. I shall indicate these several aspects, they may include as below:

On artificial intelligent invention brings high unemployment to low skill employees aspect, from the time the last artificial intelligence break through was reached in the last 1940s, scientists around the world have looked for ways of this " artificial intelligence" to improve technology, raising efficiency and productivity beyond what even the most sophisticated of today's artificial intelligence programs can achieve. Even now, research is ongoing to better understand what the new AI programs will be able to do, when remaining within the intelligence such as human brain. Most AI programs currently programmed have been limited primarily to making simple decisions or performing simple operations on relatively small amounts of data.

AI technological invention will bring much contribution to influence our future economic development. It had unique characteristics to compare common machines and it can help many industries to raise efficiency, productivity and improve performance as well as consumer individual self use. Such as the network is not taught to understand prose in any human sense. Instead, during its training phase, it adjusts the internal connections in its simulated neural networks to best anticipate the next word. It can be applied to read any article and understand any meaning to write any article as same to authors' mind and writing ability. For example, in the future, any one entered the first few sentences of any article, you are reading, the algorithm spewed out two paragraphs that sounded liked a freshman's effort to recall the gist of an introductory lecture on machine learning during which she was daydreaming. The output contains all the right words and phrases , not bad. So, (AI) technology can be applied to become just one more example of programs that do things thought to be uniquely human playing the real-time strategy game, translating text, making personal recommendations for books and movies, recognizing people in images and videos. But with the invention, of deep neural networks and the massive computational of the tech industry, computers improved until their outputs to longer appeared . In the future, algorithms can best humans, (AI) can help human to do any things in possible. Then, our society will encounter one automobile machine working environment. Does (AI) innovation will low skill employees lose their jobs because robotic can replace to any human to do simple jobs in any industries.

Whether machines can become sentient matters for ethical reasons. If computers experience life through their own senses, they cease to be purely a means to an end determined by their usefulness to us humans. Then our society will have many jobs which are needed to be worked by human, due to (AI) or robotic invention, it can replace human to do many simple jobs, e.g. factory manufacturing jobs, warehouse deliver jobs, public transportation , e.g. tram, train, ferry, underground train, bus etc. driving tasks, they are replaced by robotic auto driving, even pilot flying job will be also replaced to drive air planes by (AI) driving on sky impossible. Although, (AI) can help businesses to raise efficiency, increase productivity and improve performance, but it also bring these jobs to be replaced by (AI) and it will cause many people lose jobs when (AI) is invented to be applied in popular in our future societies. On business benefits aspect, (AI) can bring working efficiency and productivity improvement, but it can also bring unemployment ratio raises as the same time when employers accept to apply (AI) to replace human to any simple or difficult tasks.

So, we need to limit or prohibit (AI) invention to exceed human's extent in possible. I mean that we do not need to limit to invent any (AI) skill, but we need to concern human need to work in the same time. If (AI) was real replaced to do any simple jobs in any industries, then there are many low skill workers , such as factory workers, clean workers, drivers ,even high skill workers, such as lawyer, teacher, pilot. They will lose their jobs in possible. So, how to invent (AI) technology will influence our future global employment chance to provide us to continue to work in any organizations. So, (AI) will may bring high unemployment ratio, if it is applied to any low skill , even high skill jobs aspects to different industries in global.

On conclusion , in economist view, technology market development must need, such as (AI) invention because it can help any industries to raise efficiency, productivity and improve performance, but we need to know how it can be applied to avoid human to lose jobs, due to (AI) is replaced to do their tasks for any industries in possible. Whether (AI) invention can create jobs or bring job lose? (AI) scientists must need to consider how to invent their skill to be applied to which tasks aspect if they hope human won't lose many jobs to do in future one day.

● How to apply robotic to raise efficiency and productivity and improving performance for manufacture as well as bringing long term productive economic benefit to manufacturers?

It is one good question. Can scientists only concentrate on researching artificial intelligent for raising productivity, efficiency and improving performance to businesses aspect, so neglecting on research other scientific researching aspects? Technological marketing economy is as a play between independent individual subjects. However, it has also become clear that the notion of play has to be interpreted within a different framework than that of classical functionalism. In mainstream classical economics, interaction or exchange is understood as the effect of the ends-means rationally of individuals. Smith's sympathy –based view of man and society avoids this functionalistic reduction of interaction and exchange. For example, the utilitarian or functional aspect of , the social process of producing and distributing wealth through free exchange, is in Smith's view on part of the value and belief system which people in ordered and prosperous societies employ to give sense and meaning to their experiences.

Hence, in our business society, technology can bring marketing economic change to be better. One free technology marketing economic society must have these advantages to bring to influence our living, such as below:

It interprets and explains improving social processes of producing and distributing to business, such as (AI) skill invention , it can help businesses to improve performance and efficiency and productivities for their manufacturing aim only, but (AI) ought not be applied to replace to do all low skill workers' jobs in any positions in any factories or warehouses. So, any employers ought not dismiss all workers and they are replaced by all robotics. They will need to consider overall economic benefit. I mean that avoiding low skill workers unemployment ratio raises. For example, one factory can still keep 50% workers and 50% robotics to cooperate to work together. Because some human workers can be such as assistants to do any simple tasks in factory every teams. Human workers can discover any errors to let manager to know in order to improve in their cooperation process with robotics. So, human workers and robotics cooperation , it is more efficient manufacturing method to compare any manufacturing process is needed to finish from robotics only in any future factory or warehouse working environment. So, robotics and human workers cooperation can bring the most efficient production and distribution benefits to future manufacturers in any factories or warehouses because human can help robotics to find any error in order to improve. Otherwise, if the factory or warehouse has only all robotics to work. Although, they may bring raising productivities or improving performance and efficiencies. But they can not know whether how to improve their errors or revises their every time productive performance to be better every day. SO, the most efficient manufacturing method is that human workers and robotics cooperate to work together in any factories or warehouses.

On innovation and information economic influence aspect, one of the most important topics in economics is the economics of information. Information includes things as varied as e-mail, and even the text book you are reading. Information is a very different kind of commodity from things like pizza and shoes because information is expensive to produce , but cheap to reproduce. Because of the unusual nature of information, it is subject to market failure, so we need to develop different kinds of public politics to regulate it, the law of " intellectual property".

We are encountering the essence of economic development is innovation and that monopolists are in fact of innovation in a capitalist economy. What does the economics of information mean ? Who do we need to develop information economy? Modern economics emphasizes the special problems involved in the economics of information. Information is a fundamentally different commodity from normal goods. Because information is costly to produce , but cheap to reproduce, markets in information are subject to serve market failures.

For the production of software program industry example, the windows software, developing this program took several years and cost Microsoft many money of dollars. You can purchase a legal copy for $5. The same phenomenon is at work in pharmaceutical, entertainment and other areas where much of the value of a good comes from the information it contains. In each of these areas, the research and development to software on the product may be an expensive process that takes years. But once, the information is recorded on paper, in a computer or on a compact disc, it can be reproduced and used by a second person essentially for free.

The inability of firms to capture the full monetary value of their invention is called inappropriability. Inventions are not fully appropriable because other firms may imitate an invention, in which case the other firms may derive some of the benefits of the inventive investments. Sometimes, imitators may drive down the price of the new product, in which case consumers would get some of the rewards. Information consumers can earn these benefits when the value of an invention to all consumers and producers is many times the appropriable private return to the inventor (the monetary value of the invention to the inventor).

However, information is expensive to produce but cheap to reproduce. To the extent the rewards to invention are inappropriable, we would expect private research and development to be underfunded, with the most significant underinvestment in basic research because that is the least appropriable kind of information. The inappropriability and high social return on research can lead most governments to subsidize basic research in the fields of health and science and to provide special incentives for other creative activities. Thus, special laws governing patents, copyrights, business and trade secrets and electronic media create intellectual property rights. The purpose is to give the owner special protection against the material's being copied and used by others without compensation to the owner or original creator.

On the Internet information economic market influence hand, inventions that improve communications are hardly limited to the modern age. But the rapid growth of electronic storage, access and transmission of information highlights of providing incentives for creating new information. Many new information technologies have large sunk costs but virtually zero marginal costs. With the low cost of electronic information systems like the internet, it is technologically possible to make the large amounts of information available to everyone, everywhere, at close to zero marginal cost. Perfect competition is nowadays different e-commerce internet information business competitive feature, and any e-commerce merchants can not survive here because a price equal to a zero marginal cost will yield zero revenues and therefore no viable firms.

Hence, the economics of the information economy highlights the conflict between efficiency and incentives. On the one hand, all information ,might be provided free of charge, e.g. free e-book download, e-song download e-movie download from internet. Free provisions of information looks economically efficient because the price would thereby be equal to the marginal cost, which is zero. But a zero price on intellectual property would destroy the profits and therefore reduce the incentives to produce new books from authors, movies and songs from creators would earn little rewards from their creative activity. But with the costs reproduction and transmission so much lower for electronic information than for traditional information, so the future any electronic publishing industry 's products, e.g. e-books, e-songs , e-music, e-movies prices will be lower than traditional paper books, pack of songs and movies price, either consumers go to shops to buy them or consumers pay visa card to enter websites to buy any e-books , songs, e-music , e-movies from internet channel. Then, it will cause these traditional publishing and entertainment industries' competition to be raised because these e-publishers or e-entertainment can reduce their price to sell from their websites when their costs are nearly to zero. Hence, information technology can raise competition to the traditional publishing and entertainment industries. The traditional paper book, music, movie business merchants need to any authors or creators to help them to create any unique movies, songs, paper books to sell from their shops and they need to ensure their authors or music , movie creators won't give these creative book, song, movie products to any e-music, e-publisher, e-movie merchants to sell from their websites absolutely.

On conclusion, information technology influence any music, publish, movie creative product competitive raising to the traditional paper book publishers, music or movie publishers when many book publishers or music or movie creators choose e-commerce to replace traditional shop visiting sale method. So， it is possible to influence overall publishing and music and movie creative industries will change to e-commence consumption model. Then the traditional book and music and movie visiting stores will disappear and the online websites to these merchants will increase and their price also will reduce in global e-publishing and e-creative product consumption environment. So, information technology will bring some traditional store visiting number decreases and online merchant e-store number increases and consumers can pay less price to buy these creative products from internet.

● Information technologic software game consumer behaviors

What is information technologic software game strategy? How and why information technological game strategy can influence economic growth? I shall explain as below:

Nowadays, Macrosoft and Microcorp are the global information technological big companies. They own much market share in global information technological industry. Whether what factors influence they can still be global information technological products leaders. Why does computer software consumers still choose their products to compare other software products in preference? I suppose that Macrosoft and Microcorp, their hypothetical any software games have developed a clever new computer game that is certain to be very popular. Although Microcorp have the unique competitive advantage with its own software game engineers and compete against Macrosoft, but it can so it cheaper and better if it can hire any Macrosoft's software game engineers. So, in economic view, it needs to pay high salary (higher cost) to hire Macrosoft's engineers (labor), but Macrosoft's engineers can help Microcorp to invent any new kinds of software games to compete Macrosoft. Although, Microsorp needs to pay higher labor cost, but when it can raise its any software games' design and game playing methods to attract any game players. Then, these new and exciting software games can help it can bring many game entertainment players and then it can sell cheaper price to raise more attractive effort to win its competitor (Macrosoft). So, higher software game designing engineers (skill labor), their game designing effort will be the major factor to influence any one information technological companies in success. If one software designing company can employ one high software game designing effort profession to help it to design any kinds of attractive software games. Although, it may pay high salary (labor cost), but it have much chance to attract many software game buyers to compare that if it pays less salary to employ one poor game software designing profession. Because the poor software game designing profession may need to spend long time to research how to design any kinds of attractive game software to excite game players' playing desires in this playing software game industry market. Long time research to the poor software game designer may be one none any reward to compensate to the software game designing firm when it needs to pay long time salary to employ him. Otherwise, if the software game designing firm can accept to pay higher salary to the higher software game designer, he will have higher chance to help it to design any more attractive software games to influence game players' playing game entertainment desires. So, any software game designing companies their game designers (labor) must be the major factor to influence their business succeeds or fails in this software game entertainment market.

On the employing method hand, Microcorp can choose to include in its contracts with its software engineers that from working for another Macrosoft software company for a certain period of time if they resign from Macrosoft. A move such as this is sometimes called a preeptive move. Its propose is to alter its rivals' payoffs in order to alter their employing strategies. Preemptive moves are usually costly (high slaary), and this one is no exception. In its employment contracts makes Macrosoft a less attractive to let its old game software engineers want to leave their current employer, such as Macrosoft. As a result, Macrosoft must pay its software game designing engineers above the going market salary if it hopes their employment contracts can be continue between Macrosoft and its software game engineers.

Should Macrosoft must need to decide how to react. It can choose to fight Microcorp by aggressively advertising its game, which is costly high, but gives it a larger market share in the game player entertainment market, when Macrosoft had any one profession game software engineer(s) leave(s) his company and he/they change(s) to the another Microcorp software game designing company to work, or it can forego the expense of an advertisement campaign and simply share the market 50/50 with its major competitor, Microcorp to be partners.

Their competition has close relationship to influence economic growth because it will have many game players number to be increase if they can cooperate to be partners in success when they can design any new kinds of software game products to satisfy software game players' entertainment feeling. Otherwise, if they can not be one good partners and they only consider their every business benefits and neglect themselves business benefits. Then, their software playing games sale price can either to be reduced in order to attract any software game players when their software games can not be designed to have much new playing methods to attract many game players. Consequently, the GDP income to this software game entertainment market must reduce because any kinds of entertainment software games prices are reduced as well as the game players number is also decreasing. Due to they are the major software entertainment game suppliers in global. Any game players will only choose either Microcorp or Macrosoft to buy their any kinds of entertainment software game products to play majorly. So, their software game manufacturing and sale number must influence global GDP income increases or decreases in macro economy view. It implies that any countries technological software game industry's GDP income will depend on these both Microcorp and Macrosoft software game's cooperation relationship whether they have good or bad cooperation relationship. If their cooperation relationship is good, then they can manufacture high quality and attractive entertainment software games as well as raising sale price and exciting many game players' entertainment desires to achieve the increase to game players number aim more easily.

How to achieve their cooperation relationship more easier. I suppose that, in the software game entertainment industry, over its lifetime, the computer game will generate $500,000 in new income (income minus production cost) for all the firms producing it or its clones. Macrosoft must pay its software engineers an additional $100,000 to get them to agree to accept a contract containing an anticompetition clause. It costs Microcorp $100,000 to develop the software if it can hire Macrosoft's engineers and $200,000 otherwise. Aggressive advertising costs Macrosoft $70,000 and has the effect of giving it a 80% market share if it restricts its engineers' employment and a 72% market share if it does not. So, the fall in total market share is caused by the fact that without some of Macrosoft's advertisements. If however, Macrosoft passively acquiesces to Microcorp's entry and shares the market, then both firms can still achieve a 50% market share fairly. Hence, they must need to achieve 50/50 market share if they hope to achieve the cooperation relationship in success. Otherwise, they will not achieve cooperation relationship in success.

However, the spending advertisement factor will also their cooperation chance in success. For example, it would be more realistic to recast the Software Game as one in which Macrosoft chooses how much to spend on advertising with sales depending continuously on the amount spent. Other examples of continuous cooperation choices may include: the productive capacity of an electrical power plant; the salary to offer a prospective employee; or the insurance premium to charge a prospective policyholder. So, the amount to any of these expenditure factor will influence whether they will decide to cooperate to sell their software games products in global game entertainment market.

How and why Macrosoft and Microcorp's cooperation can influence global economic growth? It is significant that Macrosoft and Microcorp both technological software game designing companies are global the largest firms, they are doing international software game trade business to many countries and they have large market share in the software entertainment game sale market. Aside from trade based on technological gaps and software game product cycles, software game entertainment industry is dynamic in nature or game players' entertainment taste will change any time in completely static in nature. That is, given the nation's game players' playing taste and game entertainment factor, such as game playing designing technological method and game player individual playing game taste both. We proceeded to determine the nation's comparative advantage and the gains from the different kinds of entertainment software game designing supply factor and the game player individual game taste changing factor. So, any nation's software game players number will depend on these both factors to influence whether their number will either increase or decrease in the year in this global software game entertainment market. However, these factors can be changed by time, technology usually can improve any software game playing methods and game player individual playing taste will also change any time. As a result, the nation's comparative advantage also changes over time, such as when the nation has many game players lose their interest to buy any software games to play, then the nation ought not only consider how to develop its software entertainment game in the technological industry, it is right time to research any other new technological industries to develop if it still hopes its GDP income can rise in the technological industry overall aspect. Such as dynamic trade theory is still in its infancy. However, our comparative statics analysis can carry us a long way in analyzing the effect on international trade resulting from changes in factor technology, and tastes over time, such as entertainment software game case.

The growth of factors of production will also influence the software game entertainment industry development, through time, a nation's population usually grows and with its size of its labor force , such as China and India. Similarly, by utilizing part of its resources to produce capital equipment, e.g. India needs to utilize its technological resources, technological engineers and technological material can need to be used to manufacture either new software game products or computers. But, its technological resources will be shortage (both labor and technological material). So, many technological companies choose to apply more technological material and technological engineers to use much time and money to manufacture any new software game products. Then, these labor and material resources will be reduced to be spent time and material to manufacture any new computer products in the year. In this technological industry case, capital refers to all the man-made means of production, such as machinery, factories, communication and education and training of labor force, all of which greatly enhance the nation's ability to produce either computer products or software game products. So, the national will also continue to assume that it can experiencing economic growth is producing two commodities, such as software game and computer both kinds of technological products under the constant returns to scale. So, if India can not raise the rapid technical process to skill labor and supply technological material supplying number to satisfy to manufacture the enough software game and computer products to supply them to sell to any countries' playing game players and computer users every month. Then, its technological industry will lose many clients, due to it can not supply enough software games and computers number to sell to any countries.

Several empirical studies have indicated that most the increase in real per capita income in technological industrial nations is due to technical progress and much less to capital accumulation. However, the analysis of technical progress is much more complex than the analysis of factor growth because there are several definitions and types of technical progress, and they can take place at different rates in the production of either or both commodities, such as software game and computer.

Technical progress is usually classified into neutral, labor saving , or capital saving. All technical progress , regardless of its types reduces the amount of both labor and capital required to produce any given level of output. So, if India could have good technical progress to raise its technological labor skill and reducing the technological material to be used to manufacture the software games and computers. Then, it will have chance to keep the maximum manufacturing level number to software game and computer products as the same time.

Reference

Banerjee, A. Newman, A. (1993). Occupational choice and the process of development . Journal of political economy, 101 (2). 274-298.

Keating, M. (1993). The earth summit's agenda for change. Geneva: centre for our common future, viii, x, 12-13. 63-67.

Namik, S.D. (1965). The theories of economic growth, Cario: Knowledge House.